Doctrine of the Eons

Doctrine of the Eons

God's Immutable Plan

PAIGE-PATRIC J. D. SAMUELS

WIPF & STOCK · Eugene, Oregon

DOCTRINE OF THE EONS
God's Immutable Plan

Copyright © 2019 Paige-Patric J. D. Samuels. All rights reserved. Except for brief quotations in critical publications or reviews, no part of this book may be reproduced in any manner without prior written permission from the publisher. Write: Permissions, Wipf and Stock Publishers, 199 W. 8th Ave., Suite 3, Eugene, OR 97401.

Wipf & Stock
An Imprint of Wipf and Stock Publishers
199 W. 8th Ave., Suite 3
Eugene, OR 97401

www.wipfandstock.com

PAPERBACK ISBN: 978-1-5326-4483-2
HARDCOVER ISBN: 978-1-5326-4484-9
EBOOK ISBN: 978-1-5326-4485-6

Manufactured in the U.S.A.   MAY 24, 2019

Contents

Permissions | vii
Preface | ix
Introduction | xi

1. The Term "God" | 1
2. Immutable Defined | 11
3. The Eons And Its Origin | 16
4. Satan's Origin | 23
5. How Latin Affected Theology | 30
6. Hebrew Bible Rendering | 35
7. *Olam, Olamin* | 39
8. *Olam,* Repeated | 43
9. Aion αιών άίδις | 56
10. άίδις,αιών in the Greek Scriptures | 61
11. Eternal | 78
12. Hell | 84
13. Universal Salvation as Praxis | 101

Bibliography | 123

Permissions

Scripture quotations designated (NRSV) are from the New Revised Standard Version Bible, copyright© 1989 by the Division of Christian Education of the National council of Churches of Christ USA, and are used by permission. All rights reserved.

Scripture quotations designated (KJV) are from the Companion Bible, King James Version published in 1990 by Kregel Publications, a division of Kregel, INC. P.O.Box, Grand Rapids, Michigan 49501.

Scripture quoted by permission. Quotations designated (NET) are from the NET Bible® Copyright© By Biblical Studies Press, L.L.C. WWW.bible.org all rights reserved.

Scripture quotations designated (RSV) are from the Revised Standard of The Bible, Old and New Testament, copyright©1952, New Testament Section Copyright ©1946, by the Division of Christian Education of the National Council of Churches of Christ in the United States of America.

Scripture quotations designated (NIV) are from Holy Bible, New International Version °copyright©1973,1978,1984 by the international Bible Society. Used by permission of Zondervan. All rights reserved.

Scripture quotations designated (CSB) are from the Christian Standard Bible®, Copyright©2017 by Holman Bible Publishers. Used by permission. Christian Standard Bible® are federally registered trade-marks of Holman Bible Publishers.

Scripture quotations designated (CEB) are taken from the Common English Bible, copyright 2011. Used by permission. All Rights reserved.

Scripture quotations designated (HCSB) are taken from Holman Christian Standard Bible®, Copyright©1999,2002,2003,2009 by Holman Bible Publishers. Used by permission. Holman Christian Standard Bible®, Holman CSB®, and HCSB® Are federally registered trademarks of Holman publishers.

PERMISSIONS

Scripture quotations designated (ESV) are from the Holy Bible, English Standard Version® (ESV®), Copyright© 2001 By Crossway publishing, publishing ministry of Good News publishers. Used by permission. All rights reserved.

Scripture quotations designated (NASB) are taken from the New American Standard Bible®, Copyright© 1960,1962,1963,1971,1972,1973,1974,1977,995 by the Lockman Foundation used by permission.www.lockman.org.

Preface

THE POINT OF OUR inquiry is an attempt to investigate the word "eon" and its etymological usage. Furthermore we seek to make a comprehensive approach—as Kronen and Reitan argued,[1] this is not to be conflated with a fundamentalist or biblicist approach which upholds an inerrant Bible. This is does not imply unswerving allegiance to a particular conception of orthodoxy insofar as it is reasonable in the light of relevant arguments and evidence. This we seek to do in relation to the root behind the words *olam* and *aeon* and its English equivalent, eon. Furthermore we wish to approach each topic form a dialectical argument; this is intended to engage an Aristotelian approach. This is to convince our eager audience by adopting many starting points.I have sought to present a rather apologetic argument to the word "eternal." Due to a number of problems, including our faulty theology and a lot of what we considered sound biblical theology, this is often downplayed by traditional magisterial Protestant theology.

A critical look at the word eternal requires us to take into consideration the word from both Hebrew and Greek and how we use it in the English translations. We present a clear argument that this word eternal was not originally part of the original language of the sacred Scripture and that this word is limited in its duration. There were issues such as inconsistencies in how the word was used, e.g., age, forever, never, everlasting, forever, and ever; these are are unscriptural and unsound words that have been maintained through the translation of the Latin Vulgate translation of the Bible into English. Through the Greek, certain words were kept but were used discordantly.

Therefore, there is an attempt in this book to present the argument for the word eon and its adjective eonian as perfectly sound biblical words. We

---

1. Kronen and Reitan, *God's Final Victory*, 2.

Preface

are aware that this would upset the theological applecart, if you will, as this word answered the question of life and death in the eschatological sense.

Thus, we explain Satan, his function and power, and his ultimate destiny, of which we know little, and how God in His immutable plan called "the purpose of the eons" will bring an end to death, pain, and suffering. This is very difficult to understand in the realm of orthodoxy, which employs the idea that God has no plan of evil and death so He consigns it to a place where it would continue forever. This is absolutely callous, and it goes against the very grain of the God of love.

We sought to present universal salvation as praxis, that is, how can God save all men, will that not lead to fatalism, will it not lead to people doing what they want to do? Furthermore, it would lead to people saying "I could do what we want to do, because we all end up going to heaven anyway." This is not the case: not everyone is going to heaven. The Scriptures declare this! Furthermore, it would make a mockery of the God of the sacred Scriptures. We are not denying punishment, but we intend to show that this punishment is limited in its duration and it is remedial. It does not lead to endless duration of punishment. We intend to prove that it takes holy living and concerted lifestyles for a member of Christ's body, in a confessional way. We intend to engage with the idea of what it means that God will have all be saved. We are aware that salvation as praxis is different from Black and Asian theology, among other things. We may not have all the answers to why the problem of social and political upheavals exists in our world. But we hope that this book will help to provide some of these answers.

Introduction

The purpose of this book is to engage your thinking in the soteriological, anthropological, and philological concept of the word "eternal;" in this essay, I purpose to explain through exegetical trajectory how this word came about. Also we will demonstrate how the eons work through Helisgeschichte (salvific history); this would involve a philosophical anthropological approach by way of demythologisation of the grand meta-narratives of the biblical text, and this would involve, as Bultmann argued,[1] peeling away the layers of textual assumption and myths embellished through Western lens, thereby critically engaging a fresh approach to popular text. My attempt will further demonstrate how the eons are played out through administrational distinctions; this will enable the reader to apprehend the issues within the prisms of Christendom and understand what "Universal Salvation" is within the grand scheme of the divine theological posteriori.

    I am aware of my own parochial parochialism (limitations) in this regard, having been unorthodox in my own epistemology; we are met with a number of challenges, namely my interpretive voice may not be the ultimate definitive truth on a particular biblical text, not to mention my attempt to address the issues will open up an entire vesture of debate as to what this text is saying. Some of what you will encounter in the body of this essay may be subjective assumptive bias, based upon my own idiosyncratic approach to the text; though I have maintained faithfulness to the text in my interpretive approach, my outcome is different.

    This I hope will not distract the flow of thought or from what I intend to set out in this paper. As I believe that much of what we read currently has its own subjective bias, this is reflective of Western theology whose lens becomes the voice on biblical interpretation.

---

1. Bultmann, *Theology of the New Testament*, 321.

Introduction

Each chapter of the book will be leading one subject into the next, thus allowing a continuous flow of thought.

In chapter 1, attention will be given to looking at God and His character; my focus is to explain that God's character has been "Immutable," despite text that seems to suggest otherwise, and I will argue from the framework of God's immutability. For the sake of brevity, focus will not be on all of God's essential aspects but on this lone attribute.

Chapter 2 will provide a historical definition of the word "eon" and the reason it is no longer in use in the English Bibles. I will demonstrate in this chapter the etymological usage, thereby employing an appropriate philology to demonstrate reasons for its use and disuse today.

Chapter 3 will prove the rationale for the word eon in its Hebrew usage, and I will attempt to address through exegetical tasks the Hebrew text from the Old Testament. My attempt is not just to proof-text my assumptions, but to give a rather appropriate exegetical contextualisation of where the word eon is used.

In chapter 4, I will focus my attention on the Greek usage of the word *aeon*, and its usage in extrabiblical and Greek literature.

In chapter 5, I will attempt to show the root behind the word "eternal." In this chapter my argument will focus on how the word eternal came to found in our English translations.

In chapter 6, my attention will engage with the scholarly assumptions used in Western theology on the word eternal. I will attempt to critically engage with scholastic works punctured through the lens of evangelical theology.

Chapter 7 will give attention to "eternal torment" and its usage in the New Testament (Greek Scriptures). I will argue that eternal torment used in these New Testament texts contradict the word eons from an exegetical viewpoint. My polemic argument will demonstrate the misappropriation of the Greek text on specific texts employed by many of our modern translations.

Chapter 8 will discuss the synchronization of eons, worlds, and administration. I will provide a dispensational approach.

Chapter 9 will focus my attention on the anthropological argument on human freedom in relation to divine Sovereignty: does God really know all? Is all really determined by God? What about the argument of "Theodicy" and the problem of evil? I seek to provide some philosophical answers to the question of freedom of the will.

In chapter 10, my attention will be looking at the origin and role of Satan; I will argue that Satan, as a created being, did not originate anything as He too is a creature created by God. I will seek to develop some critical argument on Satan's origin and ultimate end.

In chapter 11, I will engage my arguments on how the eons and world synchronize in the divine economy, tabulating key points in areas of judgments and rewards.

Chapter 12 will look at universal salvation. I will critically engage on current as well as ancient patristic works on the matter of whether or not God can and will save all.

In chapter 13, I will draw my closing arguments and conclusion.

I

The Term "God"

God is supreme, all-knowing and all-wise. Who can advise Him,
or to Him dictate?

None is like Him, or, so glorious so great. His name is written in
the star-filled skies, And all in the earth His power unerring lies …

JOHN ESSEX

THE TERM "GOD" IN our society is viewed with suspicion and ire, the plethora of reasons ranges from agnostics, atheist, "don't do God," "which God are you talking about?", and so on. Within these diverse views, God is construed as some source of kinetic energy, a force, a power, or a mere object of worship (veneration). Within the creeds of Christendom, Western theology has conceived, contrived, and propounded their own idea and concept of God, which the indigenous peoples of Africa and South America know little of.

However, it is through colonization and slavery that a new conceptualization of God was imposed upon non-Europeans, when speaking of non-Europeans, what is meant is all non-Caucasians indigenous to European culture. This notion of God took on divergent forms from anthropomorphic conceptualization of the master and slave; God therefore was interpreted in a rather different hermeneutic lens from that of the slave or those who were colonized. The name of God differs in Africa from Shango, Oncolo-Colo, Ptah, Amon-Re, and Baktomare. Consequently then, the

Doctrine of the Eons

notion of God did not have a Judaic denotation, as it was not seen through the prism of Western thinking, to which end the idea of God would of course be different. How different? That depends on Jewish monotheism (or henotheism) and African polytheism. Were all Africans polytheistic in their veneration of a deity? This still remains an anthropological debate regarding how indigenous people from one side of the continent worship God. It is construed through the lens of Western theology that what is called worship from an African or indigenous Southern American or Chinese, was perceived as backward and somewhat primitive, to which end the western view of God was seen as cultured and civil.

What then do we make of the idea and notion of God from the lens of a conceptual African concept of God? Was there a monotheistic aspect of worship? I assume there most probably there was, albeit, much of the history of Africa has been decimated by internal wars, tribalism, feudalism (through village chiefdom) and transatlantic slavery. I am aware of the limitations of an in-depth research on this subject, but this is not the subject of my inquiry; we merely purpose to tabulate the issues involve when speaking about God in the Caribbean as well as to Africans. We must be aware that their concept of God was imposed on them, therefore this will not do justice in this book with the limited scope of research on this topic of God. As this is not what I intend on doing, but merely on highlighting the problematic issues when speaking about God, we are met with a barrel of anomalies. This would include conceiving the idea of God as a man, in some aspects; there are others who conceive God as a benign old man with white hair and steel blue eyes in a rocking chair. The Western concept of God can be seen through the woodcuts and the Renaissance paintings of the sixteenth century, and not only in arts and science, but also in philosophy and theology and the likes. Desiderius Erasmus (sixteenth century), the French humanist tutor of John Calvin, standardized the Greek text of the New Testament. It must be born in mind as aforementioned that Africans at this time were not seen as humans but rather sub-humans with no soul, with the brain of a baboon, therefore it was inconceivable to think of Africa ever having any concept of God from a Western lens.

Therefore when we speak of God from the Hebrew definition, the Judaic concept of God must be understood—this Hebrew Semitic root term where the idea of God is conceived and venerated. The word, *al*, has its semantic cognate roots in the Hebrew, which Jewish rabbis translated as what was construed as a semantic term meaning of the divine name. From

The Term "God"

its vowel points to consonants, the Masoretic scribes inserted the dagesh lene, which is the hardener of the Hebrew word, and this changes the pronunciation and also changes the vowels into consonant. Therefore, *al* with the dagesh lene would sound like EL, the name commonly used for God; it was also the Semitic name for the chief pantheon of deities in the religion of Canaan.

On account of that, the original Semitic people called Hebrews borrowed the idea of God from their neighboring communities in the region of Mesopotamia and Asia Minor. It was not an inconceivable notion by any means that the Hebrew people—who became the children of Israel—would borrow from the groups that surrounded them. From the biblical records, evidence shows that flirtation with Canaanite and other cultures' deities was commonplace, and the entertainment of polytheism as educible, as it brought down wrath from the chief deity. This is not the lens to which conservative theologians see the Hebrew Old Testament, as Walter Bureggemann postulated[1] that there are no secondary causes in the Hebrew Bible: any situation or event that happened to the children of Israel was because God allowed it to be so!

Ergo, the idea of God ought to be born in mind that God is not a mere object of worship as some may assume; in spite of it been used in non-biblical conversations, the term God is really unknown outside of the realm of biblical reference, and while much has been made of other alternative faiths and religious expressions, however, little is mentioned about the God of the Bible in those alternative faiths. Apart from our theological trajectory, God remains an inconceivable entity only enjoyed by religious nuts and fanatics, or so it seems today when a cultist concept of God is viewed within the parameters of individual self-veneration. Cult following with all its pomp, pageantry, and glory, and individual self-enterprise have created a God besides the Supreme Being. This then, is the God of postmodernism. It is not the fact that God is dead, so they say, it is the fact that God ceases to exist in the retention of the mind of individuals, as such human beings have made a choice to serve themselves; a popular refrain is "This is my world, I created it for myself."

Therefore the Western hermeneutic lens of God has been distorted by commercialism and consumerism, while within the Afro-Caribbean context, Blacks (I am speaking of pockets, small marginal elements that is still gaining adherents) have developed their own imagery of God, which has

---

1. Brüggemann, *Prophetic Imagination*, 62.

taken on diverse forms and approaches; there are some who call themselves "Conscious movement" and employ a method of invoking their ancestral Gods. There is also Pan-Africanism, other movements, and the self-help gospel of self-reliance, like the Nation of Islam, which holds to the view that the Black man is God and that God came in the person of Master Farad Muhammad. He spent years looking for the original tribe; everywhere his feet tread there was revolution; he found Elijah Muhammad in North America, who became his messenger, and taught him the science of eating, the knowledge of self, and what must be done in three years, then disappeared. Within the Nation of Islam there is a trinity embodied in their précises: Allah, Master Farad Muhammad and Elijah Muhammad. It was in 1967 that Clarence 13X broke away and formed the 5 Percent Nation, exclusive to the lyrical genre of the hip-hop world, where they teach that "know that every 2500 years the Gods die and a new God is born, that only 5% of those who know that the truth of God that he is not a spook but he is the Black man of Asia and the rest are deft dumb and blind."[2]

Then there was Haile Selassie (Negus Tafari) of Ethiopia. The trinity in the theology of Rastafari is Marcus Garvey the messenger, Haile Selassie the Son, and Jah the God. The sacraments are smoking herbs, as the healing of the nation which is looking to go back home, to repatriate back to Africa, to "Zion": Ethiopia. Most of the adherents of Rastafari do not see Selassie as God, but as David; the greater Son is a name only ascribed to Jesus who is dubbed "the blue-eyed boy" from Nazareth; but the incarnate Jesus for today on the other extreme is Prince Emmanuel the prophet, Marcus Garvey the teacher, and Selassie the God. Within the realm of Nihahbingi veganism is mandatory in dietary laws, another offshoot of Rastafari.

Then we have the ancient Egyptians, who hold to the view that their mother is Isis, the queen of the earth, Re is the God of the universe, or Amon-Re; many followers view the mystical pyramids as the height of their ancestral heritage, and that the hieroglyphs hold the key to eternal life; for example, the inner knowledge of self is called the "third eye." Our claim that our forefathers were the ancient builders of North Africa is problematic, because there are no historical records to authenticate this hypothesis; also, it is clear that Egypt and its surrounding regions possessed a highly structured and developed civilization in the pass. This of course was destroyed and the names of the deities of the pass was chipped away by the Greeks in their conquest of that region; the Romans, and then the Europeans,

---

2. Knoch quoted in Strauss, "Form, Function and the "Literal Meaning" Fallacy," 160.

The Term "God"

replaced the names of African deities with European ones. Furthermore a clear example of this is the theology of immortality, which was inscribed on the walls of the tombs of Egypt, which became known as the Book of the Dead of Egypt; this was developed by the Egyptians and taken and finetuned by the Greeks and Romans, who later borrowed and redefined Zeus, Hermes the winged messenger, and Hades the god of the underworld, also known in Christian theology.

Consequently then, when we are speaking about God to anyone, we need to be mindful that they may not exactly be thinking in Christian concepts, or know what we mean when we say God. So then, in our present discussion about God, we need to be sensitive about the idea of God. The reason is, the cultural trends shift from generation to generation, and with that in mind there is an erosion of any concept of thinking of some supreme being of some sort. This book will not provide all the philosophical answers to the above, as more in-depth research would be required to buttress my assumptions, so then, it is imperative when speaking about God the Deity that we consider our assumptions we seek to impose. In this book I purpose to set out the Judaic and Christian God, which reflects my predilection. The reason for this is that, as aforementioned in the my opening prefatory, the term God being a mere object of worship sets the precedent for the rest of this chapter. We are aware that Western theology remains the *sine qua non* for thinking about the Supreme Being; the reason is that in spite of postcolonial transatlantic slavery, the Semitic term God remained part of the lingua franca of indigenous Africans in some shape or form. This is based on some historical records that go on to demonstrate that God remained part of some of the indigenous people of Africa, while some were Muslims that believed in Allah, so the unitarian concept of God remained central in some of the tribal groups that transverse across the Atlantic ocean.

So, why God? In order to fully answer the question, it must be borne in mind that God—the Judaic Christian idea of God—was not borne in a vacuum; however, the God that reflects my idiosyncrasy is based on the inspired records (the Bible). The God of the sacred Scriptures operates in the realm of faith, which is a metaphysical activity; this is the reason for the why of God, we reason that within each individual there is genetic wiring that governs our propensity to venerate an object we term God. This may be construed as anything that we pontificate and genuflect to an object of worship; this in some sense is true, albeit the records of holy writ further testifies to this, as it is noted in Luke/Acts when Paul parleys with

Doctrine of the Eons

the Epicurean and Stoic philosophers concerning the unknown God (Acts 17:18–28). Interestingly enough God remains unknown and unknowable to the masses of dark unintelligent minds who grouped around in darkness, hoping that they might haply find Him. The Apostle Paul further elucidates this: *"we ought not to be inferring that the Divine is like gold, or silver, or stone, a sculpture of art and human sentiment"* (Acts 17:29).

This then is the reason given for "why God?", as it sets the tone of what we mean when we speak about God; we are not inferring that God is some disembodied spirit that pervades the universe without any real objective or goal, but we infer that when speaking of God outside of our philosophical assumptions. Theology proper postulates the existence of God, therefore, as Aquinas argued in his "Five Ways" or proofs for the existence of God—he postulates from motion, efficient cause, possibility and necessity, gradation of being, and design. His theological post-mortem arguments set the tone for Western thinking in respect to God.

Evidence of Scripture not only provides the existence of God. On the contrary, it sets the onerousness of which philosophical and theological trajectories propel. It ought to be borne in mind that as Berkhof, a reformed theologian of the nineteenth century, opined, *"The possibility of Knowing God has been denied on many different fronts. In such examples however, this denial is fundamentally equal to the assertion that man cannot fully comprehend God."*[3] This is true of course. It is not comprehensive knowledge to be able to fathom the infinite depths of the Divine being. However, while we can know God to some measure, His knowledge is nonetheless real and true knowledge. Reformed theology holds that God can be known; however, it is impossible for human kind to have a knowledge of him that is exclusive and perfect . . . (That is, knowledge of God is limited, as we are finite beings and as such our capacity to know God is therefore limited). Hodge asserts this in his argument where he infers that our senses can see things in their right perspective.[4] The question is whether the existence of God is an intuitive truth? Hodge further infers *"It is one of those truths that the mind is forced to assert. In other words, has its characteristics of universality is made a citation of intrusive truths, it is intended to apply too those truths on which have their foundations or evidence in the constitution of our nature."*

---

3. Berkhof, *Systematic Theology*, 21, 22.

4. It cannot be doubted that is such knowledge that the soul is so constituted that it sees certain things to be true immediately in their own light. They require proof. Humankind needs to be told or taught that the things perceived are true. Hodge, *Systematic Theology*, 190, 194.

The Term "God"

Consequently then, as Calvin asserts, *"Therefore it is utterly vain for person, to say that religion was invented by the subtlety and craft of a few to hold the simple folk, to thrall by this device and those very person who originated the worship of God for others did not in the least believe that nay God existed."*[5]

Therefore when considering the aspect of the existence of God, we must consider that the proof for the existence of God can be a daunting task when we fail to take into consideration the philosophical and theological implications. But is this the case? Paul Tillich postulates *"God transcends every being and is totally of being-the world."*[6] Tillich contends that there are no breaks between the finite and the infinite as far as God is concerned, as his transcendent being surpasses all of that. So then, our proposal in this chapter is not merely to provide the existence of God per se, but to elucidate the meanings and function of the name God, by purveying the name of God and His function within the course of human history.

The term God has been misused and abused through discordant renderings and from diverse biblical translations; this of course has hampered a concordant method of understanding the biblical text. Mark Strauss argued that a consistent concordant version could not be done, that is, a syntactical lexical concordance as a version could not be done; he argued that such a translation is obscure and gibberish.[7] Strauss has made an invaluable contribution to choice of biblical translation, but at best it is subjective to his own evangelical proclivity lens, i.e., what is considered to be a readable and literal as well as formal or dynamic equivalent translation.

It's true enough that most of our modern translations have made great strides to present a holistically sound and consistent translation for the target audience which they serve. However much of the translation that we have, have conveyed the idiosyncrasy of the theology that they expostulate, whether reformed, conservative or liberal, thus the concept of God

---

5. Calvin, *Institutes of the Christian Religion* (trans. Beveridge), 43, 45.

6. Being itself is beyond finite and infinity, otherwise it would be conditioned by something other than itself. Tillich, *Systematic Theology*, 263.

7. Knoch argued that since every word of God was inspired, a translation should keep as close as possible to the original words of Scripture. Quoted in Strauss, "Form, Function and the "Literal Meaning" Fallacy," 160.

Doctrine of the Eons

is hermeneutically articulated through the lens of Western theology with little regards for the Sitz im Lebem of the text.

Therefore we argue that the Greek word God [*Theo's*] is rightly construed as "Placer." Vines offers no solution,[8] nor does Mounce's expository dictionary on New Testament words offer any real interpretive answer to the Greek word or its Hebrew counterpart.[9] The Hebrew (*Al*) *El*—bearing in mind that *El* is in fact the word praise in the Hebrew based upon syntactical analysis of the Hebrew alphabet—is most often misused, as it was replaced by the Masora much later. Notwithstanding the word *al* is construed as Disposer and Subjector, and these are God's names that he is known by throughout the course of the eons. That is, the terms Subjector, Placer, Disposer, and Arbiter are relative and not absolute; they are the titles that reflect His character during the course of the *eonian* times. We will talk about the eons later in this book, but for now as a precursor, let us just say that this refers to the times of the ages.

As Placer, He is God of matter, time, and space, for he fills both time and space; He arranges in order objects and things, according to His Divine purpose and plan which He has in view. This is called in theological terms divine sovereignty. As Subjector, He both places and brings under His Divine control all owing obedience and allegiance to the dominion of Himself. As Disposer, He distributes and put into place all His creatures. As Arbiter, He directs, arranges, and appoints in making a decision according to the council of His will. This He does by adjudicating the affairs of mankind or He decides on the affairs of humanity what is beneficial and appropriate for His creation.

It must be borne in mind that this "Trinity" of titles are not permanent; however, the names Al, Alue, and Alueim anglicized by the Masorers as El, Eloah, and Elohim are the titles and are not names in themselves. These titles reflect the Judaic-Christian God throughout the *eonian* times and through Israel's cultic following. These titles are shared by the lesser subjectors throughout the course of the eons, which is His divine operations within the confines of human history. God is Subjecting and Placing people and things according to the decretive council of his will, which is conducted in and through lesser subjectors: in the First Testament they are called Malik, or messengers termed angels, and two are called Elohim. His spirit is revealed though these subjectors; they act for him. This is called

---

8. See Vines, *New Testament*.
9. See Mounce, *Complete Expository Dictionary*.

The Term "God"

"Subordinationism." Now many biblical scholars would argue that angels have free will, therefore they have the volition to do without any internal or external compulsion; this argument to some may seem plausible, too some it may seem unsettling. If I might add, the subject for inquiry in this regard would require additional research, and as this is not the focus of my attention, we merely tabulate the scholastic trajectories that are out there. The quest in my inquiry is dispensational, to which some evangelical scholars would argue that such an approach is unsound and no real biblical scholarship could be attained from this approach. We contend that appropriate investigative approach to the biblical records is not merely having a high regard for the sacred records, on the contrary, but through painstaking investigative approach to scholastic engagement.

Consequently then, when we are speaking of Elohim, we are merely seeking to assert that this is not a name contrary to current dogma, but this lone title reflects the amplitudes of His Majesty, and it reflects not just the Supreme Being in His divine singularity, but it is a title used by messengers termed angels as aforementioned.

Therefore an idiomatic translation of Genesis 1:1 would sound rather awkward to the eyes and ears of those who would transliterate the first line like this: "*Created by the Many Subjectors were the heavens and earth . . .*" Problems with such a rendering would be taking into consideration the Hebraic nuances of the text; it would be difficult to transliterate the first line of Genesis 1:1 this way but the difficulty can be overcome by the many newer translations who have recognized the difficulties, and sought to bring fresh light in their rendering of the text. The Net Bible for example states: "*This frequently used Hebrew name for God (elohim) is a plural form. When it refers to the one true God, the singular verb is normally used, as here. The plural form indicates majesty; the name stresses God's sovereignty and incomparability—he is the "God of gods."*"[10]

This then is the basis of my argument, that this Alueim is the Subjector Supreme. He is the one appointing and arranging things and objects in accord with the council of His knowledge (His Omniscience as He knows all). Angels are in fact messengers, whether they have a soul or whether they have free will is not the basis of the argument, rather, the mere fact that angels are "messengers" shows that they subject the creation into bondage (Rom 8:18–28) in order that Al or El the Subjector Supreme would receive the ultimate glory! The Lord Jesus Christ also possesses these titles, as he

---

10. http://classic.net.bible.org/passage.php?passage=Gen%201:1-3.

is the Father incarnated in the flesh in the Greek Scriptures (called Second Testament). He holds all these titles during the course of the eons, and He too is Subjecting and Placing the entire creation back to Himself, the only God and Father who will bring the entire creation to Himself, resulting in Him being all in all (1 Cor 15:24–28).

Thus Christ at present is doing the subjecting and placing during the course of the eons. For these are His titles during the course of the eons as aforementioned, It is important to emphasize that the divine names and titles God uses are in fact only used for the purpose to which He intended, that is bringing the entire creation back to Himself as I will demonstrate later on in this book. God describes Himself as the Son in the Greek Scriptures (Second Testament), as He is saving and subjecting all to Himself. As To-Subjector, He is subjecting all to the Supreme Deity who will be all in all. This may appear contradictory as the Father is in the Son and he is doing both the subjecting and placing in His church which is His body; but this is the compliment in which all in all is being completed for the entire creation as well, in accord with the council of His will.

Both the Father and Son are relative titles in both the First and Second Testaments as to our knowledge of God; it is incomprehensible, therefore in understanding the relationship with the Father and Son we need to understand the function of these titles as they serve as a precursor for salvation and reconciliation. They are necessary as He functions as Disposer and Arbiter (or Judge), one who makes a decision and rights the wrong though the decision He makes. This is called "judgment" to accomplish his intention. This brings us to the idea of immutability. What does this mean in relation to God and what does it mean in relation to what he intends for humankind? Is God immutable, and in what sense is he immutable, when conflating biblical text suggests otherwise? How do we contend with these alleged discrepancies found in the Hebrew First Testament? What does change and what does not change when discussing the supreme deity?

2

Immutable Defined

GOD IS WORKING IN his divine council to right those wrongs of mankind; God will be subjecting all of His creation, both animate and inanimate objects, to the ultimate and full adoration and worship of Himself. This may lend itself to the idea of binitarianism: the subject of subordination that is—as 1 Cor 15:20–28 asserts—the relationship between the Father and the Son is one of sender and receiver, and this act is relative as it merely spells out the relational aspect of what the Son is doing during the course of the eons. The subject is the argument of redemption and eschatological salvation.

Therefore in our quest for understanding who God is, the question can be asked, can God change? Scholars offer diverse polemic arguments to suggest that God does change and can change! Concerning soteriology God remains immutable, ontologically speaking.

In this final quest to redefine through philological and philosophical asseveration, we seek to define through philology the word "immutable;" it is derived from its Latin roots: immutablis, or "unchangeable." Immutable is the opposite of mutable, which is construed as changeable. To be immutable is to be unchangeable, not liable to change or possess variation. The "im" prefix in the case is equal to in, or "not" and is used before words beginning with b, m, or p, which was conveyed by the patristic scholars and by the philosopher Christian Wolff. He divided metaphysics into four parts: ontology, psychology, rational cosmology, and theology;[1] during the era of academic rationalists, the Post-Leibnizian school were cognizant

---

1. See Wolff, "Existence of God."

that the morpheme "metaphysics" had come to be used in a more inclusive sense than it had once been. Christian Wolff attempted to justify this more inclusive sense of the word by this device: while the subject-matter of metaphysics is being, being can be investigated either in general or in relation to objects in particular categories. He distinguished between "general metaphysics," or ontology the study of being as such, and the various branches of "special metaphysics," which study the being of objects of various special sorts, such as souls and material bodies.[2] He does not assign "first causes" to general metaphysics, however: the study of first causes belongs to natural theology, a branch of special metaphysics. It is doubtful whether this maneuver is anything more than a verbal ploy. In what sense, for example, is the practitioner of rational psychology (the branch of special metaphysics devoted to the soul) engaged in a study of "being"? Has a soul a different sort of being from that of other objects—so that in studying the soul, one learns not only about its nature (that is, its properties: rationality, immateriality, immortality, its capacity or lack thereof to affect the body), but about its mode of being, and hence learns something about being? It is certainly not true that all, or even very many, rational psychologists said anything that could plausibly be construed as a contribution to our understanding of being.[3] This term employed was known as *Saientia entais quanteurs Enis* (or the science of the essence of things: the branch of science that looks at the attributes and condition of being in general). The ontological mode of argument that the North African scholar Saint Augustine held.

Note that the perception for our senses are different and conditioned by our subjective apprehension; among these are the mathematical truths such as 3+7=10. Here too belongs the higher metaphysical truth, truth in itself, i.e., wisdom (vertas, saientia).The absolute truth, however, which is necessary, demanded by the human physic, is God himself. This is necessarily demanded by the fact now expressed, the fact which remains true: God cannot alter in His course and plan of action! This *self-existing* atom of life and light of which consists of protons and electrons, this disembodied, incorporeal, un-originated being, pervades the universe by the amplitudeness of majesty dwelling in absolute inaccessible light as recorded for us in James 1:17–18: "*Been, the Father of lights, in whom there is no shadow*

---

2. See Wolff, "Existence of God."

3. *Stanford Encyclopedia of Philosophy:* https://plato.stanford.edu/entries/spacetime-bebecome/.

from revolving motion. By His intention, He teems forth us by the words of truth . . ." (CLNT).

His solitary spirit (John 4:24, Rom 11:36): From out of the triple darkness of the womb of Space, bounded by His infinite perfections, He went to work producing the emblem of His assumption (Hebrew 1:3). The Divine expression (John 1:1): from Him came the original creative work (Col 1:15–16); He created the nine planets and the sun, which strikes the earth at a distance of ninety three million miles, by the ray of light of one hundred and eighty feet per second, making four dips thereby giving us our four seasons. This perpetual, rhythmical motion pulsates in perfect equilibrium, according to His grand and immutable design.

The ancient philosopher Ocellu Lucanus theorized that this world existed from eternity. Aristotle appears to also embrace this same theory. Aristotle a pupil of Plato postulated "heaven and earth animate and inanimate beings in general, were without beginning."[4] He further opined that his hypothesis was that the universe was necessarily the eternal effect of a cause equally eternal, such as a Divine Spirit, which, being at once power and action, could not be idle. He admitted that a spiritual substance was the cause of the universe, of its motion and form. He further stated positively in his metaphysics that God is intelligent (*ruach*), incorporeal, immovable, invisible, and the prime mover of all things. Chamberlain argues on immutability of God from the standpoint point of the love of God, that is that the love of God remains constant.[5]

According to Aristotle, the universe is less a creation than an emanation of the Deity. Plato argued that the universe is eternal (*aionias*), an image of the immutable idea or type, united with eternity with changeable matter, or a type, united with eternity. Limited immutability, we often argued in light of relative passages of Scripture, seems to suggest that God alters His position; in light of relative passages of Scripture those eisigetical interpolations of proof texts suggest that God alters His position, that is in terms of anthropomorphism (ascribing to God that which belongs to human and rational beings).

Therefore to suggest God repents or regrets, as recorded in Genesis 6:6, is an anthropomorphic idea of making God human, or we can say of

---

4. Stevenson, *Time and Eternity*, 10.

5. "To say that God is unchanging is to say that His love is unchanging. His love will pursue sinners even into outer darkness and draw them form there back to himself" (Chamberlain and Allin, *Every Knee Shall Bow*, 54).

Doctrine of the Eons

condescending or humanizing God; in other words, making God more human-like and relatable. Therefore to really appreciate God, we must understand His immutability, sovereignty, and His divine contrivance, as it is conceived and propounded within the sphere of motion that Newton received from God: when in the confines of the law of gravity, within those spheres it is governed by an immutable law of cause and effect. He the Supreme Subjector, is the self-absolute source and cause of all, for nothing is arranged or promulgated without this law being in effect, thereby bringing into motion even the most infinitesimal speck of matter called electrons and protons, which are held together by an unknown force, e.g. a stone! This imperceptible power has its cohesion in the Son (Col 1:19) when brooding over the immutable Alueim (Disposer) of the Hebrew Scriptures which corresponds to Theos (Placer) of the Greek Scriptures. He is the only Sustainer of the Universe within the realm of divine revelation, as recorded for us in Job 26:7. "He hangs the earth upon nothing," Malachi answers through His divine commentary. "I the Lord do not change." Again, reading this contextually we will note that those within the community of Israel were the subject of the chapter; the context suggests an unconditional promise, that He does not change because He will redeem them (Israel). He kept His promise and He God will continue to do so, therefore He will not change. This supposed proof text will not hold water in light of what we are trying to elucidate here, but it serves my purpose in setting forth the premise that God does not change.

What we have done is to set the argument of what God we are talking about by eliminating the hypothetical notion that I am speaking of a different God other than the Judaic-Christian God. We are not discounting that other deities do not exist, nor do we disregard other cultic expression of deity, but what we proposed to argue from the get-go is that the Christian belief paints a vivid image of a Savior that was born from an immaculate conception, and that through His impeccable life, He suffered death on the cross. Subsequently, He rose from the dead, and went to heaven to return again. Thus we sought to highlight our philosophical assumptions of what immutability is, thereby providing the praxis for God who does not change! Through we approached this argument from the framework of metaphysics, we sought to engage your thinking of immutability in light of philosophy. Tillich noted that God cannot be understood as a lone being apart from other things that exist.[6] God does not change in spite of text from

---

6. "The Being of God cannot be understood as the existence of a being alongside

Immutable Defined

Scripture that may communicate counterwise, yet from a closer inspection of the text, we will note that immutable is an innate trait of his being, and changing is not the case. God is immutable, unable to alter or change (Jas 1:17–18).[7] This leads us to the point of our inquiry concerning the eons. In the next chapter I will transverse your proclivity into understanding what the eons are in its historicity, and why this word is so important when speaking about soteriology and the eschatological life and death of human beings.

---

others or above others. If God is *a* being, he is subject to the categories of finitude, especially to space and substance . . . When allied to God the superlative becomes the dimuitive." Tillich, *Systematic Theology*, 262.

7. "All giving and every perfect gratuity is from above, descending from the Father of lights, in whom there is no mutation or shadow from revolving motion. By intention, He teems forth us by the word of truth . . ."

3

The Eons And Its Origin

IN THIS CHAPTER WE are attempting to provide the praxis for a workable definition of the word "eon." we will be engaging in lexicology and philology to ascertain the root behind the word. The problems that we encountered was in the lexicology and philology behind the root meaning of the word eon, as we were faced with a dilemma. Most if not all of the concordances and lexicons reflected the current theology of fundamentalism, therefore, it was problematic to engage with exegetical works of this magnitude without acknowledging their contribution to exegetical tasks.

However, to solve the problems that we encountered we decided to engage with biblical translation, as with new translations much of the truth is hidden in the margin of the new study Bibles. As they encountered textual variants, the translating committee chooses to put these in the margin or footnote, indicating to the reader that a more literal rendering is so and so. What we decided to do to overcome some of the exegetical textual problems is to follow the lead that is employed by many of the current versions and then we will show a closer rendering of the original from more literal translations.

As for many biblical scholars, I assume they are not acquainted with the word eon, strange as seems. It is not sci-fi terminology from *Close Encounter of the Third Kind*. However, we submit that the word eon is an inferable standard word, corresponding perfectly with the Hebrew and Greek words from where its roots emerge. Another issue that we encountered was the matter of life and death: by translating this word (eon) appropriately

The Eons And Its Origin

according to the sacred original, it appeared that much of the debate on the subject of eternal torment would seem to be questionable as to its length and duration. Also, when considering whether to take a futurist view of Revelation (the book of the unveiling), the matter of the length and duration of punishment in life and death would be called into question, as well as the lake of fire and the Olivet discourse found in Matthew 25.

Therefore, in the next three chapters, we will engage you with these matters from a lexical and exegetical framework as we seek to press the matter further to demonstrate that the common usage of the word "eternal" is not what appears from the standpoint of helisgeschichte (salvific history) from Genesis to Revelation. We will also seek to emphasize that the Hebrew word צלזמ, םלזצ and the Greek Αιοως (Αιωονς and Αεοωνιζ) transliterated eon, *eonian*, are logical biblical words from the inspired records.It is argued by some scholars, that one cannot used this word consistently through the biblical text! Granted, we are aware that context determines the meaning of the text, but to suggest that the inability to translate consistently the word *olamin* and its Greek equivalent *aionian* into English—from eon singular, eons plural, and *eonian* adjective—is absurd. Robert Girdlestone showed some interesting insight as to how this word is employed in his *Synonyms of the Old Testament* (Girdlestone's work is equivalent to Trench's *Greek Synonyms of the New Testament Dictionary*).[1] Girdlestone contends that the word *olam* should be used with the subject in mind; however, he posits the view that *olam* is in fact "endlessness."[2]

---

1. One of the most frequently words to mark duration is *ad* [עד, ass, adu] which is represented in English by the words eternity, ever, everlasting, evermore, of old, perpetually, world without end. This word is once used where there is reference to past duration of a limited extent, namely, in Job 20:4. It is used as a state of being which is at once past, present, and future, with regard to God who inhabits eternity (κατοίκων τόν αιώνα) (Isa 57:15). It is applied to the endless duration of God's reign (Exod 15:18, Ps 10:16) where the LXX is very string (εις τον αιώνα και επ αιώνα και ετι); to the throne of God (Ps 45:6), to the Messianic kingdom (Ps 89:29); and to duration of God's righteousness, praise, and commandments (Ps 111:3, 8, 10). See Girdlestone, *Synonyms of the Old Testament*, 312.

2. Eternity or endlessness, and this idea is only qualified by the nature of the object to which it is applied or by the direct word of God. When applied to things physical, it is used in accordance with the revealed truth. When applied to God, it is used in harmony with the truth that He is essentially and absolutely existent, and that as He is the *cause causarum* and without beginning so in the very nature of things it must be held that no cause can ever bring an end to His existence. When the word is applied to man's future definite and after the resurrection, we naturally give it the sense of endlessness without limitation, except such as the post-resurrection state shall involve; and this not revealed. See Girdlestone, *Synonyms of the Old Testament*, 317.

Doctrine of the Eons

Fundamentalist Christians (biblicists) would argue that they do not see it as being an issue to engage with, however, we beg to differ in that when speaking of judgment, punishment, rewards, and losses, the subject of the eons becomes the *sine qua non,* and when speaking about anthropology, haematology, soteriology, and the life of God. It is the quiddity under which the entire theology of Scripture is underpinned.

Ergo, within the constructs of post-modern skeptics—those who superficially read and argue that truth is relative and one cannot arrive at real truth because everything is relative—will not be able to appreciate the God of the Bible, or the truth that is contained in the inspired original. Francis Bacon (1561–1626) argued *"Whosoever shall entertain high and vaporous imaginations instead of laborious and sober inquiry of truth, shall beget hopes and belief of strange and impossible shapes."*[3] This is the trend of modernity; as truth becomes subjective, therefore, one cannot arrive at any real truth, but painstaking investigative interrogation of the Hebrew and Greek Scriptures will assist the student of the Bible to unravel, from research buried in a pile of ologies, some aspect of truth.

From this sonnet, we can deduce what we mean by eternal. High up in the land called Svithjod, there is a rock. It is 100 miles high and 100 miles wide, and once every 100 years a little bird comes to this rock to sharpen its beak. When the rock has been worn away, then a single day of eternity will have gone by. This apocryphal narrative with its variations has been around for centuries in philosophical and theological circles; this is just to demonstrate how long eternity is. John Stuart Mill (1806–1873) is quoted as saying, *"there is no subject on which men's practical belief is more currently indicated by the words they used to express it, than religion."*[4] Even Darwin cautioned, "false hypothesis was as dangerous as a false observation. A false hypothesis may at least advance the organization of material; but everything that is based on false observation has to be completely undone before we start again."[5]

---

3. Bacon, *Essays.*
4. Mill, *Liberty,* 121.
5. See Charles Darwin's *The Descent of Man and Selection in Relation to Sex,* 1.1.

SUPPRESS THE TRUTH AND SUGGEST THE FALSE!

In jurisprudence, *supressio veri* is deemed an offense equal to *suggestio falsei*. Yet some biblical scholars commit this very offense when they suppress the true by suggesting the false. This is true in regards to the interpretation of words. All too often our understandings of words are based upon our embedded scholastic trajectory and assumptions, which are already developed from our theological training or lack thereof.

For this reason, it is imperative that when it comes to interpretation, we are aware that translating committees have a high regard for Scripture, and so do we. We infer that when this word eon came about, it was Adolph Ernest Knoch and his coworkers who first discovered this word, saw the inconsistencies in our English Bibles, and through his love and high regard for Scripture, painstakingly went to work to discover what is in God's Word, the inspired original, thus to translate from the donor to the receptor language or target audience. Yet, such committees translate within the framework of embedded theology, such as from a Reformed or Arminian position, or a liberal or conservative position. The embedded lens to which Scripture is often viewed have become somewhat tinted, therefore, it is important to hold a sound hermeneutic to Scripture. We honor the Scriptures and the God of the Scriptures, so we must possess a solid understanding as to the authorial intent and the divine intent (listening to the voice of the text through the promptings of the Holy Spirit). We must possess competence in order to better understand what is behind the text, in the text, and in front of the text. This is made facile with the used of concordances, lexicons, Bible dictionaries, and other useful tools.

Therefore in considering the approach to interpretation of Scripture, we note that lay Christians assume when reading the sacred text that they understand what is read. There is a tendency to think of our understanding as being the same as the Holy Spirit's, or the human author's, intent. However, we invariably bring to the text all that we are, with all our experiences, culture, and prior understanding of words and ideas. Occasionally, what we bring to the text, unintentionally to be sure, leads us astray, or else causes us to read all kind of foreign ideas into the text (eisegesis). This is especially true when considering the word eon.

Biblical scholars convert an unpleasant fact into a present non-fact; they suppress the truth about the eons (which they deem an unpleasant fact). By suggestion of the false (the pleasant non-fact of eternity), Aristotle's aphorism is appropriate: "the larger the island of knowledge, the greater

Doctrine of the Eons

the coastline of ignorance."[6] The dense darkness which shrouds this subject can be banished only by God who says: "*Out of darkness light shall be shining He shines in our hearts with a view to the illumination of the knowledge of the glory of God in the face if Jesus Christ*" (2 Cor 4:7).

The doctrine of the eons is crucial to our understanding of God's plan and purpose in relation to Christ, the cosmos, and its creatures, within the sacred Scriptures. God does not make sin endless, nor death eternal, nor estrangement everlasting, nor punishment forever. The mere fact that the First Testament is written in Hebrew with some Aramaic, and the Second Testament Greek Scriptures were composed of koine Greek, implies some difficulty in understanding. However, our English Bibles are very different; had it been originally rendered in simple, native English alone, it would read quite different. It is also true, that a large bulk of English words that were employed, were borrowed from their European continent, and some from our ancestors from within the continent of Africa, Asia, and the North Americas . . .

Consequently then, and more importantly, there is the mere fact that most of the important theological terms and idioms were adopted either from Greek or Latin. When asked, "What is the most important subject in Scripture for the sinner?" many would answer "salvation," yet this important term only came into use in the English language about the twelfth century—say 800 years ago. This term was purely a Latin word, as Latin was the only lingua franca known. At that time it bore the meanings both of "safety" and "health;" in fact the word salvation occurs only once in the Anglo-Saxon Scripture (680–900 CE) or in Wycliffe's version, he employed the word "health" although he employed other terms like "make safe" and "safe," but also "heals." Tyndale, in 1526 CE, was the first one to use the word salvation in Scripture, he used it only once in John 4:22, "Salvation is of the Jews." Wycliffe had "for health is of the Jews;" therefore, the fine English of Tyndale had "health" dropped out, and was completely displaced by the imported but now important Greek word, "salvation."

Eternal is also one of the many words which gained entrance in the English translations, instead of maintaining the Greek and Hebrew word *eonian*. The Greek word was lost, so they could have used the Latin word *ece*, German *ewig*, Dutch *eeuwige* . . . in fact it may be laid down as a rule that no language had for some time after the first century possessed the term "eternity." This is not widely known, however it ought to be noted that

---

6. Rosen, Stanley. *The Philosophers Handbook*, 18. New York: Random, 2000.

The Eons And Its Origin

hypothetically speaking if the older Bibles that were Latin were translated from the Greek, the outcome would have been different! If the Latin Vulgate of Saint Jerome (380 CE) was not in existence it is highly probable that the word "eternal" would have never been in our Bible, as aforementioned with its antecedent theological trajectories. However, it was due to the Norman conquest of England in 1066 CE by William the Bastard (William the Conquerer) with his hordes of people from Normandy, that brought French words into the Danish and Anglo-Saxon words. At this time English was a somewhat substandard vernacular, and furthermore it was not as glorious as Latin, so the French brought their words into the English language of the Anglo-Saxons and Celts. French being a largely decayed corrupt form of Latin, this drove out the native English words; it must be highlighted that English words were developed by the Danish, Germanic tribes, of the Goths, the Visigoths, and the Saxons, who were the first settlers of England. We should now be using not eternal but *eke* or *weg*, the old German equivalent of *eonian*.

On the other hand, had it not been for the hordes of Turks who sacked Constantinople in Asia in 1453, the likelihood is that we would have had the Greek term *aeonian* incorporated into English instead of the Latin to further buttress our argument. It was the Turks who captured Constantinople, and that was of enormous importance to Europe. It was then that the great center of learning, especially in places like Antioch, Alexandria, and Syria, and all those important centers for learning Greek and the classics, were destroyed. It is hard to believe that for over a thousand years up until the year 1453 CE, Greek became unknown, in fact, forgotten in most of Europe. In fact no Greek was taught publicly in England until about 1484 CE, when it began to be taught at Oxford University. Erasmus, the Dutch scholar, learnt Greek at Oxford and subsequently was professor of Greek at Cambridge from 1509 until 1514, during which time William Tyndale was a student. It is said that Erasmus standardized the Greek text by producing in 1516 the first Greek New Testament; in so doing we have heard of the wet ink comma put under the menz door of Erasmus's room for the Johannine text; as the legend goes a scribe who rewrote 1 John 5 inserted the comma in the Greek text, and put it under the door of his bedroom in the morning. Erasmus inserted it into the John text to support the doctrine of the "Trinity."

Erasmus then issued his first Greek New Testament, the first Greek grammar in over a thousand years. It was published in Milan in 1476 and the lexicon four years later in 1480. It was standard for years to come. Centuries later, A.E. Knoch (1874–1965) and his coworkers painstakingly spent forty years to discover the Scriptures in its original language; they sought to bring to the public a translation that would be faithful to the original language by doing exactly what Erasmus did centuries ago: standardize the Greek text with the Greek interlinear and Greek elements, to demonstrate to others that you can have an idiomatic translation that is faithful to the original Hebrew and Greek.

4

Satan's Origin

THERE HAS BEEN INSURMOUNTABLE ink spilt on the issue concerning Satan's origin. Furthermore, the issues have been compounded by the ecclesiastical proclamation by the diverse Western churches as to the definition of Śātān. Attempts have been made to make his origin as some perfect being that, through some sinister motive and so-called free will, subsequently fell. The origin of Śātān has been met with half-truths, myths, fables, and, to some extent, outright lies regarding his existence. We seek to draw your attention to some important issues in this chapter that seek to link the origin of the eons, the term immutable, and the basis of the meaning of the eons, which will enable the diligent reader to tabulate the reason for Satan and what purpose he serves in the grand scheme of things.

In understanding the origin and activity of the śātān-adversary, it would be helpful to initially understand the function of messengers (termed angels), their functionality, and how that serves as a framework to highlight the role of the śātān-adversary in the purpose of God. It must be borne in mind that the initial existence of evil spirits are clearly the intention of God's will.

Job 1–2 provides the only instance in the Old Testament where God and the śāṭān converse with each other; twice God initiates the dialogue by asking the śāṭān a question about his whereabouts (1:7; 2:2). The question answered, God proceeds to bring Job and his impeccable spiritual credentials to the śāṭān's attention (1:8; 2:3). The śāṭān is not impressed. On the contrary, he suggests that Job's motives for serving God are selfish ones; i.e., Job serves God to get what he really wants, which is prosperity. Thus the śātān directly impugns Job's motives for service to God and indirectly accuses God of divine patronage. The śātān's question to God is a thoughtful, legitimate, and profound one: "Does Job fear God for nothing?" To disprove or substantiate that question, God grants to the śātān carefully circumscribed destructive powers (1:12; 2:6). The śātān cannot not act independently, but only with divine permission.[1] Job 26:13: נדה בהש שפדה בדזהך שממ הדפה הלילה ש יבש: Greek: Κλειθρα δέ οὔρασυού δεδικασιν αὐτόν πoοσταγμτι δέ ἐθανάτωσε σράκοντα. Ἀποστατής. The Septuagint version: *"By His spirit he made beautiful the heavens and His hand travailed as He formed the crooked serpent"* (translation mine). The Hebrew חללה is the masculine adjective meaning slain, pierced, mortally wounded, and profaned. The thought of the serpent as fleeting or piercing mythical figure is quite illuminating. For the Hebrew *yâsar* is a verb meaning to form, to fashion, to shape, to devise, which is also found also in the LXX, slaying the ἀποστάτης "dragon." The LXX adopted this term, which eventually evolved into other mystical meanings of the "Grnogise" for his actions! When these events occurred is not known in the sacred records. Nor are we specifically told what caused the rebellion and what caused Śātān to be in the lower region of the heavens. Hints of this are seen in other texts of the Hebrew Scriptures, that the aluiem fought with the śātān in the creating of the heavens and earth; again this hint is seen in text like Isa 41:1–2. But this is not our line of inquiry.

Because of this frustrating silence, Western evangelical scholarship has often gone off on a theological tangent, contorting discordant ideas and hypothesis in trying to find the origin of the Śātān and his rise and fall. This information is not given; all we have are legends and myths that are foreign to the sacred records. He was an angelic creature, a rational superhuman in power, and created by the supreme Deity.

Furthermore, Ferguson and Wright posit the idea in the *New Dictionary of Theology* "that within Christian theology the notion of a devil has its origin in the OT."[2] Śātān is one who "obstructs" or "opposes," the meaning is carried into the Greek: *Satanas* or *diabolos* (devil), the chief designation

---

1. Freeman, *Anchor Bible Dictionary*, 1234.

2. What Ferguson and Wright meant is that the notion of the Devil is understood as an "adversary," which is a literal meaning of the Hebrew "śātān." Wright et al., *New Dictionary of Theology*, 197.

of this evil power in the New Testament.³ The noun śāṭān occurs 26 times in the Old Testament. Seven of these (discussed above) refer to terrestrial śāṭāns, thus leaving 19 references to celestial śāṭāns. Three of these 19 use śāṭān without the definite article (Num 22:22, 32; 1 Chr 21:1), the remaining occurrences are in Job 1 and 2 (14 times) and Zech 3:1–2 employs the noun with the article (haśśāṭān), literally "the śāṭān." Leaving aside Num 22:22, 32 because there the angel of Yahweh is a śāṭān, we note that 16 of 17 references to the celestial śāṭān use the expression "the" śāṭān. The lone exception is 1 Chr 21:1. This would seem to indicate that only in 1 Chr 21:1 is śāṭān possibly a proper name.⁴

Smith Bible Dictionary suggests, "he was angelic in nature, a rational and spiritual creature, supernatural power, wisdom and energy—an archangel, prince of heaven."⁵ Śāṭān is the name given to the prince of evil.⁶ The anglicization of the Hebrew common word שׂטן the Śāṭān and the feminine form-שׂטנה-Shitnah coming from the verb שׂטך (śāṭān) meaning to resist or to be an adversary is used six times in Scripture. The noun has been etymologically related to a number of germinate third weak hollow verbs which we do not find in the Hebrew and its cognate languages. Some have proposed the meaning of the verbs as "to stay,"⁷ but that Śāṭān root definition is not as some Western Christians think. Note, the root of Śtn is not evidenced in any of the cognate languages or texts that are prior to its contemporary usage, i.e., that occurrence meant in the Hebrew Bible. The

3. Mills, *Lutterworth Dictionary of the Bible*, 798.

4. Freedman, *Anchor Bible Dictionary*, 1230: śāṭān does not appear in Genesis 3; later rabbinic sources identified śāṭān with the serpent in Eden (Soṭa. 9b; Sanh. 29a). He is identified in a more impersonal way with the evil inclination which infects humanity (B. Bat. 16a). In a more personal way, he is the source behind God's testing of Abraham (Sanh. 89b). Additionally, śāṭān is responsible for many of the sins mentioned in the Old Testament. For example, it is śāṭān who was responsible for the Israelites worshiping the golden calf because of his lie that Moses would not return from Mount Sinai (Šabb. 89a). He is the driving force behind David's sin with Bathsheba (Sanh. 107a), and it is he who provokes the gentiles to ridicule Jewish laws, thus weakening the religious loyalties of the Jews, Yoma. 67b.

5. *Smith Bible Dictionary* (Peabody, MA: Hendrickson, 1986), 591–92.

6. *New Dictionary of Biblical Theology*, 1064.

7. The root term has often been linked to two ancient root terminologies: Arš Her ŚTH, ETH Šty, AKK šatu 1and SyrST, meaning to revolt/fall away, to be unjust; AR Šyt, to burn; Syr SWT and Ar šTT, burn. These purposes required discounting the *nūn* of the noun Satan as part of the root, and attributing it an •-ân suffix. Firstly, the ân suffix when apprehended to a normal base normally results in an abstract noun, adjective, or diminutive. Toorn, *Dictionary of Deities and Demons*, 256.

noun Śàtān is employed as a divine being in four contexts in the Hebrew Bible. Num 22:22–35: Balaam, a non-Israelite seer, set out on a journey, an act that incurs God's indignation. God responds by dispatching his celestial messenger, the *msal'ak yhwh* described as Śātān, who stations himself on the road upon which Balaam is traveling; Balaam is ignorant of the sword-wielding messenger but the donkey sees the danger and twice avoids the messenger, for which Baalam beats the animal. The messenger then moves to a place in the road where circumvention is impossible. The donkey lays down, and is again beaten. At this juncture Yahweh uncovers Balaam's eyes so that he can see the sword-wielding messenger, and Balaam falls to the ground. Most scholars attribute this narrative to the J-source, which would have made it apply to a celestial being. However, since the narrative is dated in the sixth century BCE or later, with the exceptions of the above story, which is obviously ridiculous, Balaam is characterized in an extremely positive way in Num 22:24. Outside the chapters, the first clear indications that he is being viewed negatively are attributable to P9 Num 31:1) and Dtr2 (Josh 13:22), both of which are typically dated to the sixth century BCE. This suggests that negative views of Balaam likely stem from a later source. As we can readily see the heavenly being, Śātān in Numbers 22, has very little in common with conceptualization of Śātān. Who is Yahweh's messenger, not the mimesis, who acts in accordance with Yahweh's will rather than opposing it? Of course, Yahweh's messenger elsewhere in the Hebrew Bible is hypostatization of the deity.[8]

This suggests the view that the Deity is in fact there in their personification of the serpent, to dupe the first human to join. If this is the case, it would contradict the later revealed truth of Satan's subsequent end. The adversary is real! There are those who affirm that music was built in him, and he once led the heavenly choir, but now we cannot say if there much truth in that. However, it ought to be noted that the "Lucifer" reading was inserted into the Scriptures by Western theologians in order to hoodwink readers into thinking that Śātān was once perfect, and through some sinister motive enacted a *coup d'état* resulting him being kicked out of heaven! We put it to the reader to observe that God is not like a human person nor does he possess human tendency; if Satan was once perfect, then, what made him sin, what motivated the adversary to draw a third of the messengers in heaven? If 'The Śātān' was perfect, and through some sinister motive fell, then the fault is in the lap of God, which would be construed

---

8. Toorn, *Dictionary of Deities and Demons in the Bible*, 726–27.

that as God's sin, and that He had made a mistake in creating something "perfect" that actually had a flaw in his disposition. This is not the truth; God is perfect and has no flaws in his divine operations.

Are we are to charge God with sin? Banish such thoughts for it would border on blasphemy, as God cannot sin or make a mistake, nor is sin found in the supreme Deity. Śātān is considered a figment of the human imagination, though this is assumed because he is not a part of the celestial host yet possesses aerial jurisdiction, that is, possesses suzerain over the sons of disobedience. Yet he has access into the presence of God to be a tempter of mankind.

Job 26:13 refers to the beginning of Śātān and Isaiah 14 refers to his eschatological end.[9] This occurs at the consummation of the eons, when death is abolished and Christ conquers the one who has the power of death, the Śātān, who was created a crooked metaphorical serpent from his inception that God had travailed in, as His hand formed him—this extended metaphor is like a woman traveling before giving birth. Śātān did not originate anything; he is a creature for only the very purpose that he was created for: to be an adversary. To further buttress this argument, we contend that God has the right over the clay.[10] God created sinning messenger-angels in order to make His powerful contrivances known, God carries with much patience vessels of ignition, adapted for destruction.[11] The New Testament also makes frequent references to Śātān; he is mentioned by name 35 times. The breakdown of these references is: (a) the Synoptics, 14 times; (b) the Gospel of John, once; (c) Acts, twice; (d) the Epistles (all Pauline and half of which are in the correspondence with Corinth), 10 times; and (e) Revelation, 8 times (5 of which [2:9; 2:13; 2:13; 2:24; 3:9] are in the letters to the churches and not in prophetic portions [chaps. 4–22]). As popular as the designation Śātān is, the name *ho diabolos* appears 32 times.

There are additionally a number of titles given to him. For example, while John uses Śātān only once (13:27), the preferred Johannine term for Śātān is the "prince of this world" (12:31; 14:30; 16:11). This phrase parallels Matthew's "the prince of the demons" and Paul's "the god of this eon" (2 Cor 4:4), "the prince of the power of the air" (Eph 2:2), and "rulers of the darkness of this eon" (Eph 6:12), but not "rulers of this eon" in 1 Cor

---

9. See also Rom 16:20: "And the God of peace shall crush Satan under his feet swiftly . . .

10. Rom 9:20–24.

11. Rom 9:22.

2:6–8, which refers to human rulers. A Johannine parallel appears in 1 John 5:19 where the claim is made that the whole world is in the power of the "evil one." These references teach at least a modified dualism which is close to the Qumran picture of a titanic struggle between the angel of darkness and the Prince of light.[12] The evangelist (John) references the devil in 8:44. This could not refer to the time prior to Adam's existence, rather the text suggests that it occurred when the Śātān was introduced to our first parents in the "Good World" of Adam's day. The Śātān is described in the Greek as a "man-killer, from the beginning." This testimony in itself could not be referring to activities prior to the creation of man. Hence from mankind's inception, the Śātān has been the opponent-adversary of people. This form of anthropomorphism, of man in communion with his Creator, is a reflection of how will be in the oncoming eons when again resumptive fellowship with God the Father will be restored. Death will not be the subject in the "Good World," nor every pain and other ills, for it would be considered sheer utopia.

It should be made clear that Śātān does not have vaticination, nor is he omnipresent, he can only be willed by a greater authority, that is God; as such, he is interested in the affairs of cosmic and world governance, and not in human activities. The faulty theology held by certain sections of evangelical Christianity would have it that the Śātān is everywhere at the same time. This in fact is incorrect and it should be borne in mind that the host of demonic influence foisted upon mankind clearly explains the reason why Christians misunderstand the demonic influences under the power of Śātān, by interchangeably employing it. It cannot be denied that Śātān is involved, for he gives power and life to these demonic forces. However, it is indirect rather than direct.

With this in mind, we can deduce then that as a creature, he did not originate anything, as a creature he is in the hand of the great Potter, and as such, he is controlled by a power that restrains him, the power of the Holy Spirit; further, he does not possess free will, he cannot do what he wants without divine permission, as I have said.

Will šātān be saved? No! Salvation is between mankind and God, wrought by the vicarious sacrificial work of atonement on the cross by Jesus Christ.

Furthermore I will argue that reconciliation will involve animate and inanimate aspects of creation. Will that involve Satan? We are not told

---

12. Freedman et al., *Anchor Bible Dictionary*, 1040.

implicitly or explicitly, and it is difficult to arbiter, though patristic apologists Origen, Gregory, and others made a case for this. Reconciliation of śātān the adversary-opponent of mankind will serve its purpose that will lead to the abolition of death, and the complete subjection of all.

With this in mind, attention will focus on the issue of how Latin has affected our theology in the way we understand the doctrine of soteriology.

5

How Latin Affected Theology

IT MUST BE NOTED at this juncture, as Thomson argued,[1] that classical Latin was singled out as one of the many languages of that day during the fifteenth century. Its root was found in 454 BCE in Italy, when Romans expressed a desire to establish and codify their laws. They sent out commissioners to Greece to study the laws of Solan of Athens, which then became the elite lingua franca of the region of Latium. It was not originally the native tongue of the people, even as classical Greek of the poets and the dramatist was not the common dialect of the everyday people. The language of everyday Greek was *Koine*, or "common;" Latin was the language of the patricians, of the literary world, of the politicians, of a comparatively minute section of people. It came to reside in the position of a partly artificial dialect amid other widely differing dialects.

It is important to highlight some important points. The Roman conquest of "Africa," which was the ancient region of Kermit ruled once by the Canaanites who had a colony there at Carthage—from which Augustine hailed from—in North Africa, near Tunis. This coloney was founded by the cities of Tyre and Sidon and some have sought to identify Carthage with Tarshish, but this is not the case! History records three long wars known as the Punic (Phoenician) Wars, which took place between 264 to 146 BCE, ending in the complete subjugation of Carthage, which then became a province of Rome. Therefore, Latin became the dialect of the time up until the second century BCE. Carthage became an important center for Rome

---

1. Thomson, *Whence Eternity*, 26.

in spite of its distance. It however spoke a different Latin than that of Rome itself.

Tertullian of Carthage (160–220), the Latin father who exhibited the earliest form of Latin, which was different from the classical Latin of Rome. Hence the distinction of the Latin of Rome from the Latin of Carthage continues for quite a long time. Hence while the old Scriptures remained in North Africa, they continued with little or no change, whereas upon its arrival in Italy, the Romans had new Latin words and idioms which were different from that of North Africa.

Hence the rise of Jerome who was given the arduous task of attempting to bring about harmony from the confusion, and the result was the Latin version, from the thirteenth century onwards, that was known as the Vulgate. Jerome, nonetheless, in his revision, while correcting apparent errors and setting right what appeared to be in his view "bad" Latin, was very conservative otherwise. Many expressions he left as he found them. In any event Jerome did not appear to have revised two Latin words, fraught with profound significance, which he found in the old version of Tertullian. From the word he found that rendered the Greek word *aeon* into Latin, like Gothic and Armenian and English, necessitated two words: *speculum*, from which we have discovered our root word "secular"; and *aeternus* from which came down the fateful words "eternal" and "eternity." Sometimes as we note, the Greek *aiōn* (eon) was rendered by one of these two Latin words, and sometimes by the other.[2] The famous council of Trent, in Italy, sitting in from 1545 to 1563, decreed that "This same ancient and Vulgate edition, which by the long use for so many centuries has been approved in the church itself, is to be upheld as authentic in public readings, disputations, sermons and expositions; and no one dare or presume to reject it under any pretext whatever."[3] The words used for "centuries" is *saceculuorum*, or speculum.

---

2. Seculum is defined in Latin dictionaries as meaning a generation, an age, the world, the times, the spirit of the times, and a period of a hundred years. That which is secular pertains to the current world, notably to the world as not spiritual. The French word has come to be construed as a century, besides meaning an age, period of time, and world (*siècle*). The future *siècle* is the "life to come." Seculum is sometimes derived from the same root word meaning "sequel," meaning time as "following." Thomson, *Whence Eternity*, 11–12.

3. See the full text at: https://history.hanover.edu/texts/trent/trentall.html.

Doctrine of the Eons

Thus the basis of our argument is to provide a historical rationale for the word eon and that the historical development in our English Bible is questionable. As it is met with a number of theological anomalies, what was the intention of the translators when they ignored the Hebrew and corresponding Greek term in order to translate this very word the way they did? What was the agenda, if there was one? As we are all aware, all translations are in fact interpretation in some form or other. Therefore, much of what we do know and do not know of the original still remains contestable.

I am seeking to purvey some sort of praxis that the translations that we have and laud are essentially flawed when translating this word; also the Hebrew and Greek lexicons are evangelical and are oscillated by the so-called orthodoxy within the echelon of evangelical theology. To further buttress this argument, Bauer's *Greek English Lexicon* noted the word αιωϛ as time.[4] Not once is there any confusion as to this word, as it signified only a period of time. Moulton and Milligan's *Vocabulary of the Greek New Testament* states *"that it is period of time an age, a lifetime. In general, the word depicts that which is the horizon is not in view, whether the horizon be at an infinite distance or whether it's at one span of life."*[5] In leading evangelical *Dictionary on New Testament Theology*, Colin Brown does not give a definition of the word Αιον from the New Testament (Second Testament), but he provides scholastic trajectories, that through his own epistemology, provides theological dictum that this word Αιων does express endless duration when speaking about the rewards and punishment and the life of the dead.[6]

According to the infamous magnus opus of Gerhard Kittle in 10 volumes— as we know from many Greek scholars who have highlighted the fact that its first four volumes were codified, and in any event, it still stands paramount

---

4. A very long time, or a time gone by, a segment of time, age, nearing the end. Bauers, *Greek-English Lexicon*, 27–28.

5. There are thee collateral declensions from the same word. These are from the Sanskirtayu and its Zen equivalent. The idea of *life* and especially long life, predominates. So with the Germanic cognates (Gothic *aiws*). The word, whose root it is of course futile to dig for, is a primitive inheritance from Indi-Germanic days, when it meant "long life" or "old age"—perhaps the least abstract idea we can find for it in the prehistoric period, so as to account for its derivative. Moulton and Milligan, *Vocabulary of the Greek New Testament*, 16.

6. Brown, *Dictionary of New Testament Theology*, 196.

as the vanguard for translating Greek words—"everlasting," or "eternal," was the term used for existence; it became rare during the time of Hellenism, but it was brought back to use by the Stoics.[7] Kittle is not helpful in this vein as it does not engage the matter with clarity, but obscures the meaning with philosophical trajectories. According to Robinson and House's *Analytical Lexicon of the Greek New Testament*, in its word entries enters the word as "an age, a cycle (of time) of the present age, as contrasted with the future age, and of a series of ages stretching to infinity. The adjective αιώνς is age along. Therefore, partaking of the character of that which last for an age . . ."[8] This is a much closer definition of the meaning of this word than of the old *Vocabulary of the Greek New Testament*. Again Mounce adds period of time, life, character, an era, an age, hence a state of things making an age or era; the present order of nature; the natural condition of man, and the world.[9] It appears that all the lexicons and concordances all correspond to the Hebrew word *olam* and its Greek equivalent *aeon*.

What Moulton and Milligan sought to provide from the framework from which the origin of this word is derived, is the concept of beyond the horizon; this is the idea which asks the question of where the eons is concerned. It is a long duration of time. The matter of judgment and life and death we will talk about later; at this point in time, we wish to engage you by pressing further our point on this matter.

We will return to Colin Brown later, as at this juncture it would behoove us to recapitulate the aforementioned statements that we have elucidated. We have highlighted that this Hebrew word *olam* and its Greek counterpart *aeon* from the get-go did not express endlessness in the early development of the English Bible; we sought to understand through the standardization of the Greek text that the Hebrew was also obscure, and most of the translators relied on the Greek version of the Hebrew text.

We also tabulated that the Greek language was lost for over a thousand years. Therefore, it was difficult to convey the original language, when in fact the known language of the day was Latin, and Jerome's Latin Vulgate, which was the standard gold medallion of the day in translations of Scripture. Furthermore, as we have noted, and as we will show later when we go further in looking at this etymological usage, we will discover that the word eternal was replaced but it did not come from the Greek word or

---

7. Kittel, *Theological Dictionary*, vol. 1, 172.
8. Robinson and House, *Analytical Lexicon of the New Testament*, 12.
9. Mounce, *Complete Expository Dictionary*, 53.

Doctrine of the Eons

even the Hebrew word; as a matter of fact, this word was invented to shore up a theological hypothesis concerning the life of the dead, rewards, and punishments.

Consequently then, we will be looking at how the church fathers saw this word and why was this word repudiated as it was; also we will be arguing that the word eon transliterated from the Hebrew and Greek is in fact a sound word for those who have a high regard for the sacred Scriptures. We will now in the next chapter engage your thinking into the Hebrew usage of the word; we will look at the First Testament text and what they say concerning the judgment and life; and we will look at the word eon's meaning: is it limited or does it describe endlessness? Thus, what we have provided in this chapter is the historical template of the origin of the word eon; granted, much of this has been hampered due to a lack of resources in this area. Suffice to say, what we are contesting is that from a historical standpoint this word did not convey the word as it is currently taught.

6

Hebrew Bible Rendering

IN THE LAST CHAPTER, we sought to provide a historicity beyond this word, eon. We attempted to show that the word eon was lost because there was no Greek that was known for over a thousand years and even worse, it was the result from the Hebrew. We sought to show you that, according to Willem A. VanGemeren, the word was a *"normative, denoting a long time,"* the root was unknown.¹ He further suggests that *"it furthers when used in the Old Testament as 'the farthest time, distant time. It does not seem to mean eternity in the philosophical sense of the word (i.e. neither unbounded time nor eternal endlessness), although they may be few verses that suggest such.* סלזע *usually describe events extended into the distant past or future. Such distant time is clearly relative."*² Therefore, we can see the most prominent evangelical dictionary clearly describes that this word *olam* is in fact a word that does not express endless duration, but in fact demonstrates that it is limited in its scope; in fact, it also shows, with the Greek vocabulary, that the word itself is limited in scope and that it does not reflect eternity. How sure are we that the VanGemeren hypothesis is correct? The BDAG Hebrew lexicon agrees with VanGemeren that the normative masculine denotes "long duration."³ Holladay also argues that the Hebrew suggests continuing

---

1. Hidden, so that that basic meaning of the normative, as suggested by the Aramaic cognate alam; would be qatal. This form is unattested as mom. Base in a Semitic language. Consequently, it has been suggested that the—am ending of the nom. Is an adverbial ending and not part of the root. VanGemeren, *Dictionary of Old Testament*, 346.
2. VanGermeren, *Dictionary of Old Testament*, 346.
3. Long duration in antiquity. Brown, *Hebrew and English Lexicon*, 761.

Doctrine of the Eons

future, always.[4] He did however, concede that the word when in an ancient text suggests the idea of eternal and forever, yet from the word entry, it is clear that from the get-go, it did not express endless duration as it is commonly assumed. The *Analytical Lexicon to the Septuagint* says it is used as a masculine normative singular noun denoting lifetime, life, age, generation, long space of time, age, eternity, world, ages, and eternity.[5] Much of the entries are in fact discordant renderings, notwithstanding the idea that the word עלם and its Greek counterpart αἰώνα as it is found in the Greek Old Testament (Septuagint) did not express endless eternity as it is assumed by evangelicals, but on the contrary, it expressed a long duration of time. May I ratiocinate further, that as a notable biblical writer elucidated from both Testaments and the Greek version of the Hebrew Scriptures, the word עלם in Hebrew is derived from a primitive root meaning to "veil from sight," to "conceal."

Vladimir Glelesnoff opined, "*A conspectus of the Biblical text proves that the word 'Olam' expresses duration, the whole time during which a person lives, a state that exists.*"[6] This further may be rendered correctly in an interpretive sense, if not essential meaning by any term expressing the duration required of the noun *olam*. According to the Companion Bible's reference appendix, it can suggest *"'to hide,' 'hidden time,' of which occurs over four hundred and forty eight times in the Hebrew Bible First Testament.*"[7]

From a young creation perspective, Adam, will eventually have an end. עלם—*olam*, when used of persons, can be expressed in terms of a whole life or lifetime, a succession of generations, or the state of people, or creation, rather than a period of time or an extended period of time, commensurate with specific application (e.g., Prov 22:28, Gen 6:4, Ps 77:5, 143:3, Josh 24:2).

Olam certainly refers to periods of time, and when considered contextually, cannot be rendered as it does in our modern translations as forever, everlasting, or even eternal. Such discordant renderings should be expunged from our translations, when speaking of the life and death of resurrection and judgment. The Psalter, the twenty-fourth division (Psalm 24), is the triumphant antiphonal anthem which was sung to celebrate King David carrying up the ark; the song demonstrates what we are talking about

---

4. Holladay, *Concise Hebrew and Aramaic Lexicon*, 264.
5. Tayler, *Analytical Lexicon to the Septuagint*, 18.
6. Knoch et al., *Unsearchable Riches*, vol. 1, 10.
7. *Companion Bible KJV*, appendix, 151, 175.

after the capture of the ark back from Jebusites' city (2 Sam 6:12–19); verse seven and nine reads: דִינְפ סלזע "life up your head gateways and be lifted up." סלזע *Olamin* is transliterated *eonian*. CVOT has verse 9 as: "Lift up your head gateways, And be lifted up portals [*eonian*]." In the Septuagint, the Greek has από τον αιώνος and in verse 9 ητε Νταλί αιωιοι "arche doors anionian." The word *arche* sound like the word for ancient or decadent. The Revised English Bible has "everlasting doors" as does the KJV, however the new translations like the ESV (English Standard Version) has "O ancient doors" followed by the CEB (Common English Bible), NIV (New International Version 2011), NSAB (New American Standard version 1995) RSV (Revised Standard Version), NRSV (New Revise Standard version). The NET Bible (New English Translation) choose to use the Hebrew word *olam* and its Greek antecedent "eternal," strange as seems. Why the translating committee chose to translate this Hebrew word remains suspicious. In fact, when the Hebrew interlinear confuses the two Hebrew words by rendering the word *olam* סלזע דלמ אדביך as "me" makes it highly confusing, and the mere fact that the translating committee made a decision to translate it to "ancient" adds to the confusion. We understand that to translate a particular text from the donor language to the receptor language would require translating a particular text that reflects the nuance of the receptor language, and of course while doing so you will note that in transmission much of the language would have been lost; however, some of these problem has been eliminated, but not altogether. The target language to which one would want to translate has already a predisposed theological thinking, therefore reading a new translation can be problematic if your favored text does not flow with one's idiosyncrasy.

Most translating committees would argue that the words "ancient" or "old" are a correct rendering; in this case it would help to demonstrate yet again that the same word *olam* in the Hebrew is in fact the same word used by Jonah in his soliloquy in the belly of the fish (Jonah 2:6). Was he there "forever"? or was he there for three days and three nights? It is the same Hebrew word; this makes it inconsistent as one verse has "ancient" and then another, "forever"!

Consequently then, as we have discovered from the aforesaid statements, we tabulated the important fact that if a particular word is going to be translated it ought to translated consistently. Whereas most scholars would argue that you cannot use one word to translate one Hebrew word, Concordant version said you can! Some translators say it is impossible, but

Doctrine of the Eons

the Concordant Bible translation says it can be done, and furthermore it would not affect the context of any given passage; in fact, it would actually enable us to see the text in light of its appropriate context, when considering judgment, rewards, punishment, and the life of the dead as mentioned in our introduction. Note a popular text in Exodus 21:6 reflects this; a word that the ESV interlinear translates עֹלָם "eternity," from the same Hebrew word family of *olam*, but the Common English Bible (CEB) makes a far better rendering of "he will serve him as his slave for life," and the NIV has "servant for life." The Holman Christian Standard Bible (HCSB) also made improvements on the rendering, and the Concordant Version Of the Old Testament (CVOT) says "will serve him for the eon." What we would like to highlight here is that the Biblia Hebraica Stuttgatensia corresponds to our modern translations and the Lennigradensia corresponds to the KJV, and both translate this word as עֹלָם *olam*; also the Septuagint has εἰς τον αἰῶνα transliterated into the eons.

The Hebrew slave (servant), whose ear was bored through, served as a slave for his lifetime in the singular, for the עֹלָם transliterated *olam* "eon." This applies even to Solomon's life in 1 Chronicles 22:10 and its corresponding text 1 Kings 8:13 and 9:3. We should note that at that time the temple was in existence, and there was a time it no longer existed; it did not last forever. Ecclesiastes 1:4 and Psalm 78:69 speak of the earth abiding "forever," and when compared with other passages such as Matthew 5:18, 2 Peter 3:7–10, Revelations 21:1, and Isaiah 65:17, defeats the argument.

7

Olam, Olamin

THE FORMS OF THESE Hebrew words suggest a normal noun and the plural; unless there are convincing arguments to prove otherwise, we should disregard it. Psalm 61:4 says: "Let me sojourn in your tent for the eons;" the ESV interlinear has עולמים "eternities;" all the translations seem to reflect this plural עולמים *olamin* the same way as the Septuagint reflects son in the αιωνις. Again, the Greek of the Old Testament and the Hebrew are the same, they are not saying eternity or eternities.

Therefore, if we want to be sure that the Hebrew had expectation of the resurrected life in some state, which is represented figuratively by "the tabernacle," we ought to have grounds for regarding this statement as approximating to endless future bliss in heaven! If we take this verse literally, we will still find difficulty, unless we regard *olamin* as having connotations similar to those of עולם, which is used frequently as, for example, "possess constantly till the end of one's life." This passage may well be understood as a pious aspiration, of longing to practice in the presence of the God for all of one's days. The note on NRSV is quite illuminating as it appears to be a plea to be in God's temple.[1]

In any event, the "dwelling began in this life" so it cannot be "eternal" in Psalm 77:5. The psalmist employed poetic hyperbole, or exaggerated statement, by expressing the state of depression. "I took account of the days a fore-time, the years of the eon . . ." The poet continues this lament

---

1. An individual, far away from the temple, prays to be led there and enjoy its protection and nourishment. Coogan, *New Oxford Annotated Bible*, 210.

Doctrine of the Eons

in verse 7, with a figure of Erotisês emphasizing the continuance of their introspection: "Will the Lord cast us out *la olamin*?" All the translations go against the Hebrew word *olam* and its plural *olamin*. The argument is whether or not the translation is aware of this mistranslation, or are they simply ignorant or is it because the evangelical lens are like blinkers, causing the inability to see the trees in the forest? Especially when it comes to this word. Again, Isaiah 26:4 reads "Trust in Yahweh into the futures of the future, indeed in Yah, Yahweh, the rock of the eons." This is not exactly a correct rendering. Ehat I am honing in on is that the Lord is a rock for the *eonian*, he is the *eonian* rock, and this concept is enshrined in the time-honored hymn.

In Isaiah 45:17, Israel is saved by Yahweh with an *eonian* salvation. The difficulty of the Hebrew verb tense is apparent here in this text. The use of the future tense avoids the clash with the facts within Israel's history. There seems to be no sensible alternative to "Israel shall be saved by the Lord." *La olamin*? However, of course *olamin* can scarcely be a plural of extension meaning "eternal," for obviously this "eternity" has not yet begun, in which case "Israel is saved by (in or among) Yahweh, with a salvation *eonian*. They shall not be ashamed or confounded for the future eons."

"Salvation for the eons" could be thought of as a deliverance for which Israel has long awaited. This interpretation avoids the dilemma, and therefore demonstrates the verse to be in harmony with Israel's history and prophetic expectations; this is not the evangelical or fundamentalist interpretation of this text, as we are all too aware of the Christianization of the Hebrew Bible; as a result much of the exegetical task of seeing it in its exact setting, in its Sitz im Lebem,[2] has been lost due to fanciful interpretation.

All of the text containing the plural *olamin* can be logically translated and interpreted consistently without any reference and interpretation to eternity at all. The introduction of concepts of endless time or timelessness led to incongruities in almost every case. The view that *olamin* is a normal plural signifying an extensive period of time has often obscured the dating either of inauguration or ending both; it provides meaningful renderings consistently throughout, and also the consonant within the context in each case.

Therefore, it is imperative that when considering the plural and the singular the derivatives do not express endlessness, as supposed, but are confined to a limited duration; to further illustrate this note the following

---

2. Setting in life.

text. In Genesis 9:16, the interlinear in the Hebrew again is עולם and in the Septuagint it is aionian αιωνιους. Plural in its form from the original Hebrew and Greek, clearly elucidated it does not denote eternities as it is transliterated but *eonian*, as it refers to the duration of a human life; consequently, it is limited in duration.

In Jeremiah 18:15, עולם תזידת תזיזדש,[3] the תזביתנ תבלל סלזע (verse 16) Greek of the Hebrew Scriptures reads αμτων σχοινους αιωνιους. Then how do the translators justify the word in verse 15 as "which made them stumble in the ancient paths" (NIV) and the horror of lasting scorn in verse 16? Even the Readers Hebrew Bible by Zondervan for the NIV did not correct it. The ESV has "in the ancient roads," and in the next verse the same Hebrew word is translated as "a thing to be hissed forever." We agree that the translator sought to translate for the purpose of clarity and accuracy, however, we need to see the authorial intent according to the context. Suppose we are not aware of the authorial intent or the Divine author? What are we left with? We may consider the sociological or physiological approach by trying to ascertain what the author felt and the social condition that surrounds their circumstance. Also scholars may keep in mind how that word would sound today in the receptor language. The problem with that premise is that context still reigns in the realm of text, true enough; however, we could argue that the ancient authors may not have intended what we mean today; this is the difficulty in "Readers Response." What was said, who is listening, who is seeing? To be sure we can only convey shades of the original but to disregard a word that clearly reflects time by substituting it for of old, ancient, and many other odd renderings like eternities, shows a disregard for the sacred original for the sake of appeasing evangelical fundamentalism.[4]

Consequently then, by translating it as *"And they stumble in their ways, the eonian trial"* (CVOT), it alludes to the time period in which Israel had to undergo slavery, among other things, during the 560, 587, 582 BCE Babylonian destruction of Jerusalem. In verse 16 we have *"To make their*

---

3. "And they stumble in the their ways, the *eonian* trails . . . to make their land a desolation an *eonian* hissing" (Jer 18:15–16).

4. According to J. I. Packer: this is "depicted as a religious phenomenon, distinguished not merely by its queer doctrine of Scripture, but also certain peculiarities of practice." Packer, *'Fundamentalism' and the Word of God*, 1.

Doctrine of the Eons

land a desolation, an eonian hissing," which corresponds to the context of Jeremiah's lament.

Thus, we have highlighted that *eonian*, in relation to human life, is limited in its duration; the lament of Jeremiah is one of the many examples how one can consistently translate this particular word עלם and its plural עלמים. Ergo, our attention will be turned to *olam*, in its repeated sense.

Psalm 145:13 states "thy Kingdom is an עלמים (*olamin*)"; the Septuagint (LXX) has: Η Βασίλεια πάντων των αιώνων. It is highly possible to construe this into meaning that the rule of IEUE (YHWH) is coexistent with the being of the Deity, but "all generations" suggestd that the thought of the writer is that God rules in the affairs of humankind (Dan 4:25). There appears to be no reason to think that the psalmist had any concept beyond time in mind. The literal "for all the eons" appears to be quite satisfactory. It seems apparent that these two probably tragic expressions in the poetic couplet cover the same duration of time. Evidence must be very scarce, if it exists at all, to demonstrate that the First Testament authors, even the exilic, had any exception of an *eonian* future, whether within time or timeless, in which generations of humans would go on reproducing their kind ad infinitum. What we sought to do is to take some isolated texts and by engaging them to explain that the word *olam* in the Hebrew did not express endlessness or eternal, and it should not be expressed as such. For not even the Hebrews expressed time in this sense, as they perceived time beyond the horizon.

8

Olam, Repeated

THE PHRASE FROM THE עלם and עלם and to the עלם and from the עלם and to the עלם (*olam* and *olam*, and to the *olam* and from the *olam* and to the *olam*)—these adjectives are in the superlative form in the Hebrew and are not common words that can be translated from its Hebrew origin straight into the English Bible. There are eleven examples, eight of which are liturgical. The very use of *min* (from) and *ad* (to) demands a distinguished difference between two entities. In respect to time (as of course to space) one may speak of passing "to" and "from" a single entity (see Jer 7:7 and 25:5). We might add that it is certainly not "from all eternity to all eternity" or "I have given long ago to your pass ancestors for all time" (CEB) or "Your ancestor for all time" (NIV, HCSB, CSB, NASB, KJV and ESV). The NET Bible uses forever and ever in both cases; it recognizes both idioms but does not correct them.

The text speaks of the promise of the land and its tenancy, which has a beginning in history, thus it cannot be eternal; however, it was earthly (terrestrial) in location and scope. There must be an element of devious exegesis in introducing either "everlasting" or "eternal" into these passages. Daniel 7:18: "But the saints of the Most High shall receive the Kingdom and possess the Kingdom forever and ever" (ESV). The CVOT reads "Yet the Saints of the Supremacies shall receive the kingdom and they shall safeguard the Kingdom unto the eon, even unto the [עלם עלם] eon of the eons."

The same hermeneutic rule applies. By exegeting the text in light of its context, we will note the Hebraism (Hebrew idiom) is consistent in the repetition of words. The repetition of *olam* suggests that the term did not itself represent unlimited duration, otherwise the first עלם *olam* which is a singular would have covered all the time in view. Consequently then, the entire context is oriented to the eschatological duration of time which has not yet transpired if we are to take a dispensational view of this text. An eschatological historicist view of the said text demonstrates that these events have already transpired, which leaves us with a dilemma of how would they translate this particular text in light of Israel's history.

Thus, in the phrase we have both singular (*olam*) and plural עלמים. *Olamin*, a plural eternity, is by definition an impossibility, therefore the term suggests that it's pointing to a time in the relatively obscure future. Beyond-horizon or remotest time is plausible, yet "remotest time and remotest times" is contradictory. To the remote times even a remote times would conform to Hebrew idiom, making the second phrase a normal Hebraic polytonic superlative (e.g., *Kings of Kings, Lord of Lord, Holy of Holies, Song of Songs, Die to be Dying* and so on).

Some of the scholastic trajectories opined that Daniel is late in his writing even among Jewish scholars; they do not see Daniel in light of a prophetic individual, but as a historical one! Furthermore, the Jewish stylists were masters of historical fiction. Therefore the concept of the eons and the periods of time developed. If this is the accepted view, the text may then be translated (to or for) an eon, even an eon of the eons. By treating it as "an eon of the eons" as a normal Hebrew superlative, we get the translation "Saints of the Supremacies shall receive the Kingdom and they will safeguard the kingdom unto" [or into, for the eon present, participial] even the eon impending [to come]." This is taking into consideration the last *olamin*, עלמים (eons) in the escalation that had passed into the Day of God!

From the Jewish lens, in regard to the exile, even during the present day, they envisaged eon of the eons of their nation possessing the kingdom; this has been regarded as the עלם עלם eon of the eons, or the time of restoration and promised blessings, of which the Hebrew Bible (Old Testament) has much to say!

The synoptic as stated above suggests that the development of the use of עלם *olam* in the sense of a period of a time is similar to that covered by *aion* and it is accompanied by the use of the plural *olamin*. The existence of Israel arose as a united nation somewhere around 930–1000 BCE. Eternity, without beginning or ending, is never mentioned as such as in the עלם *olam* passage, from which convincing evidence can be obtained in relation to עולם *olam* to show that the concept of infinite duration was not in existence among Hebrew scribes or writers of the Hebrew Scriptures. Therefore the words "eternal" and "everlasting" could not be used as a translated derivative of עולם *olam*.

Consequently then, from the aforementioned statements we can deduce that the Hebrew עולם *olam,* whether in the plural or the singular form, clearly depicts a duration a period of time; it does not express endlessness, or endless duration, as it is often translated. Also it ought to be highlighted that the words "ancient" and "old time" are unsuitable alternative renderings, as we have tabulated that the word cannot be consistently transliterated into the English equivalent.

Ha Olam, Olamin *and* Ha Olamin

The question of whether עולם *olam* in the Hebrew Bible ever represented a concept of an age or period of time, possessing some distinctive characteristics and is therefore recognizable as separate in some sense from another age or ages, has some importance in this attempt to discover the meaning of the above term during the composition of the Hebrew Bible.

In our postmodern times, we commonly speak of "the computer age," "the scientific age," "the age of reason" and so on, without envisaging any exact limiting date lines; the beginning and end are obscure, but nevertheless the use of the definite article and some qualifying adjective or phrase indicates the existence of the idea of a recognizable period that is in some way individualistic. Such periods often overlap, and many complex factors are involves, so precise limits cannot be determined. When we use the term eon, be it figuratively and hyperbolically, we omit the definite article. For example, "She takes an age (or ages) to choose a dress." The relatively long time, and the uncertainty of the moment of conclusion of the project corresponds as we have seen, with the majority of the Hebrew Bible cases of the use of עלם *olam*. It is common knowledge that the Hebrew Bible of the Old Testament times showed limited regard for the sort of logical systematic thought patterns that Greek philosophers are noted for. It appears both rational and psychologically sound in aspect that the concept of the eon existed, and it did not mean the whole of the time; there would also accompany it, not only the plural form of the word but also the concept of

Doctrine of the Eons

the plurality of eons. The two ideas are essentially related and supplementary, thus the one cannot exist without the other, and one presupposes the existence of the other. The argument might be set out thus:

If an eon meant duration of time such as if it meant a part of time, then there must be another of one eon: it necessitates a plurality. Normally a plural for which a singular exists presupposes the existence of a single individual entity. There cannot be more than one of the entity that does not exist as separate ones.

Furthermore, we present a list of the occurrence of the terms: עֹלָם *olam* plural from *olamin* עֹלָמִים. As we only selected a few texts, what we sought to tabulate are the common usages as to how this word was used in the Old Testament (Hebrew Bible).

ha olam	olam repeated	olamin
The noun *olam*	from *olam* to *olam*	plural
1Chr 16:36	1 Chr 16:36	2 Chr 6:2
2 Chr 17:14	2 Chr 29:10	1 Kngs 8:13
Ps 28:9	Ps 41:13	Ps 61:4
Ps 41:13	Ps 90:2	Ps 77:5
Ps 106:48	Ps 103:17	Ps 77:7
Ps 133:3	Ps 106:48	Ps 145:13
Eccl 3:11	Jer 7:7	Eccl 1:10
Jer 28:8	Jer 25:5	Isa 26:4
Neh 9:5	Neh 9:5	Neh 45:17
Dan 12:7	Dan 7:8	Dan 51:9
Joel 2:2		Dan 2:4; 9:24

As tabulated above, we note that through the selected passages of Scripture, we have discovered in every instance where the transliterated term עֹלָם *olam* and its plural form appears, we may infer that they refer to the time of its editing into the form that we have, םלוע *olam* and its plural form םימלוע *olamin* were used concurrently. In 1 Kings 8:13, םימלוע *olamin* is used in Solomon's prayer at the temple dedication. However, if these words were actually used by Solomon, that would demonstrate that the plural was then in use. It is highly probable that many of the Psalms were dated late in Israel history; a notable exception is Psalm 41, which is commonly attributed to a Davidic writing. Both the םלוע *olam* and םלוע *olam* repeated a number of times in the psalter suggest the answer to the question: Can we establish the time when *olam* appeared in writing? We may tentatively reply: Yes, broadly speaking in the days of the Undivided Kingdom. The fact remains in Psalm 41:13 we have "from olam to the olam," which implies two periods and hence plurality, and it supports the view that "the olam" and םימלוע "olamin," if not contemporary in emergence, at least were linked in usage.

Thus, the expression here, as is common with most cases of the םלוע *olam*, is liturgical; it most probably does not justify any specific statement respecting the idea behind the term. For instance it gives no indication of a beginning or an end, or any other characteristic features. Thus obscurity or indefiniteness is not to be equated with eternity; non-clarity is not equivalent to endlessness. To our second question, Does the way the םלוע *olam* is used indicate the nature of the concept represented? Yes and no, it is based upon the context, when referring to the past; the noun is often used to construct a phrase to modify other nouns. This is the reason given by some scholars.[1] However, it ought to be noted that םלוע *olam* is limited in duration when speaking of the life of human beings. As VanGemeren further argues: "םלוע *Olam refers to the future, it also refers to a future of limited duration, and that is, to condition that will exist continuously throughout a limited period of time.*"[2]

We speak about the disruption in Genesis 3: the story unfolds to show that if they take of the fruit of the knowledge of good and evil they may live forever. Did God know that this would happen? If this took God by surprise, as some scholars have suggested, we make God the author of sin, which is

---

1. As in the case of Psalm 24:7, 9 where the gates are described as םלוע pĭthê Ŏlâm, the "ancient gates." VanGemeren, *Dictionary of Old Testament*, 346.

2. VanGemeren, *Dictionary of Old Testament*, 247, the noun is sometimes used in a construct phrase to modify another noun, such as perpetual, continual, according to Prov 10:25.

blasphemous. Such a thought we could not harbor, for it goes against the grain of divine revelation which argues that God knows all things, He operates all thing in accord with the council of His will (Rom 11:36). The dilemma remains; if we take this text and carry it over to another text like the Book of the Unveiling (Revelation), then in that text, which mentions that the tree of life was used as a healing potency for the nations, the meaning is that it did not promise eternal life, but to sustain life.[3] Even in this text, no promise is made as to eternal life or endless duration, no, in the latter half of the book (Rev 22:14), *The Interpreter's One-Volume Commentary on the Bible* (Buttrick) makes a point as it links this particular text to the ones in Genesis and Ezekiel.[4] This demonstrates to us that a text may have a link in terms of reference, but it does not suggest that the tree of life promised immortal or endless life. Therefore we argue, as Stern tabulated in the *Jewish New Testament Commentary*, that the tree of life, which was removed from the Garden, is now restored, and it is this which provides nutrients and healing for the nation.[5] From said comments, we can conclude that the divine council did not infer that Adam and Eve would live forever, but that taking from the tree of life would sustain life; that is, it is highly probable that the tree of life enabled them to live for an extended period of time.

Consequently then, it would be improbable to look at a particular text like this one in the primeval creation to infer that immortality was promised to Adam and Eve, when this is not the case. On the moral ground, we could argue that the command given to Adam and Eve was a consequentialist command, that is, you will die if you do not take of the tree; then we have the counterfactual argument which is, if you do not take then you will live for long period of time (beyond horizon). The argument for immortality is not seen, as immortality was a later concept in Hebrew thought that was developed in the Second Temple period. This idea of immortality and immortal life would have not developed here at such an early period.

---

3. *Will grant to eat of the tree of life, which is the paradise of God* (Rev 2:7, NASB).

4. "Of the tree of life in the New Jerusalem the river flowed, out of the garden of Eden (Gen 2:10), and Eden's tree of life (Gen 2:9) are no doubt the ultimate source is Ezek 47:1–12 . . . it is probable that also that John thinks of it as nourishment for the dwellers of the heavenly city . . ." Buttrick, *Interpreter's One-Volume Commentary*, 968.

5. Stern, *Jewish New Testament Commentary*, 854.

To press home the issue of a lexicological argument, עלום *olam* in the Hebrew is not construed as an endless duration; much ado has been made of *Strong's Concordance*, but the problem with *Strong's* is that it is a layman index for biblical words, it is not an analytical concordance. Therefore it cannot provide an indepth analysis for this word. The case made for *Strong's Concordance* is rather weak, therefore, it behooves us to press this matter so for the sake of brevity we will revisit this word in the Hebrew and make up in our own minds what this word is meant to be. Young's *Analytical Concordance* is quite illuminating: "לגצח To pre-eminence, perpetuity, נצחים לגצח—To perpetuity, לעלם, עלום, עלם (le or ad) olam, עלם, לעולם, hidden time, לעולם-To the age, לגצח נצחים, le-Netsach netsachim to perpetuity again עד ad, duration עולם Age age-lasting."[6] From the arguments presented from Young's *Analytical Concordance*, we can deduce that the word eternal was not in the mind of the original authors, nor does it appear to be so in the mind of Robert Young. *The Eerdmans Analytical Concordance to the Revised Standard Version of the Bible* remains the best concordance for biblical words: זו, מילים, מיסידראל, לעדלם, דעל, סלדעל, דאם, חצב, דע, עלם, דע עלם. These are the words for forever, everlasting חצבל, עדרלמים.[7]

Thus it appears from the statements that the word eternal was not the authorial intent in the text, behind the text, or in front of the text. Thus the notion to express endlessness is determined by the subject applied. As Henson suggests[8] in some instances that the reduplication of עלום *olam* seems to be a rhetorical amplification of the idea, without comprehension of ages by greater ages. This is especially true when עלום *olam* is in the singular in both parts of the reduplication, as in "to the eon of the eon." The use of the word in the plural is decided upon the evidence that the sense of the word is not eternity, in the absolute sense, for there can be no such eternity. However, the passage of time and the future can be divided by eons, thus there may be many eons, and an eon of eons.[9] The Hebrew was destitute of any single end to express endless duration. To express eternity they said "before

---

6. Young, *Analytical Concordance to the Holy Bible*, 310–11.

7. Whitaker, *Eerdmans Analytical Concordance*, 323–24.

8. "The word Great is an illustrative word. Great applied to a tree, or mountain, or man, denotes different degrees, all finite but when referring to God, it has a sense of infinite." Hanson, *Greek Word Aion-Aionios*, 16–17.

9. "The pure notion of eternity is too abstract to have been conceived by any word in the ancient languages, But a cultivation advanced and this idea became more strictly developed, it became necessary in order to express it to invent new word in a new sense as with the words *etenitas, perennitas*, and so on." Hanson, *Greek Word Aion-Aionios*, 18.

Doctrine of the Eons

the world was"; to expression the future, "when the world shall be no more . . ." "The Hebrews and other ancient people had no one word for expressing the precise idea of eternity."[10]

Furthermore, when considering the phrase *ha olam*, what is meant by this, as Stevenson pointed out, is that "in regards to time, it is important to bear in mind that the element of obscurity (that which is unknown), regarding to the concept of time, do not at any time justify to the introduction of endlessness when time periods are indefinite."[11] Eternity without beginning or ending is not mentioned as such in the *olam* text of the Hebrew Bible's First Testament. Nor are there any statements among the writers of the Hebrew Scriptures from which we can demonstrate that convincing evidence can be obtained to show that *olam* as the notion of infinite future ever existed. Therefore the words eternal and everlasting should not have been used to translate from the Hebrew term *olam*.

So then can the word *olam* inform the Hebrew derivative that is used for "eternal"? Since in fact God is Spirit,[12] then we can conclude that *olam* when ascribed to him means eternal! To be sure, there is consensus in favor of the fact that God is eternal, and to say that God is a God of time, the God of this age, the God of the days of old, or an existing transcendent God who is present, does not in any way conflict with his eternal being as Deity. The God of Abraham, Isaac, and Jacob is not limited to the patriarchs by that title, nor does "the Lord of the entire earth" (Josh 3:11, 13) confine him to the domain of the earth.[13]

English is somewhat problematic when translating the word eternal; as Stevenson asserts, eternal is often used ambiguously. In the aphorism, for example, "The price of freedom is eternal vigilance," the meaning is "constant," unremitting, even "perpetual," but the duration of the being of God, with beginning or end, must be rejected, as having no relevance to the subject at all.[14]

---

10. Stevenson, *Time and Eternity*, 20.

11. The list presented were concurrences of the word *olam* developed over a period of time similar to the Greek counterpart *aion* and accompanied by the employment of the plural *olamin* which arose during the existence of Israel as a united nation around 1000 BCE.

12. John 4:24.

13. "By associating finite concepts of time or space with the name of God, we do not in any sense question or impugn His infinite transcendence." Stevenson, *Time and Eternity*, 37.

14. Stevenson, *Time and Eternity*, 39.

Olam, Repeated

Deutero-Isaiah is a designation given to the book that is broken down from 1–39 First 40–54 Second and 55–66 Third. In Isa 40:27–28, note the following: דמדאלה׳ משפט צברד הלדא׳ רצח אם לא שמצח אלה׳ ערלם ׳הזה. In the Hebrew, note that the word *olam* is underscored before IEUE (YHWH) and before Alueim (Elohim). The LXX renders it και νμν ομκ εγνως; ει μη ηκουσας; θεος αιώνος. We have sought to underscore the Hebrew word and its Greek equivalent respectively. This demonstrates to you that the translation of the Hebrew read God Olam Lord. The schema is the same word found in Deuteronomy 4; the ghostwriter is asking in the text is to assist the audience by employing a rhetorical question, but this is not speaking about a God who is everlasting, rather, it is speaking about His sovereignty against the Babylonians. God *eonian* is the subject of the text. The ghostwriter used aphorism to explain in poetic prose the power and almightiness of God. Coggins argues "YHWH personally summing those whom he wishes to do his will is characteristic of Isaiah. By contrast with the so-called gods, YHWH had made a purpose in one great panorama. The section ends with further polemic against the uselessness of other gods. This is expressed so frequently and with such vehemence in these chapters that the threat they present must have seemed to a real one."[15] It is clear from the aforementioned statements that this section of the text did not address the idea of the God of time, but when speaking of God in relation to the gods of the other nations, God indeed is timeless. The subject is not here in the text. Maybe Isaiah was struggling to express some idea of indefinite duration, but it must be doubtful whether "first" and "last" and "from the beginning" indicate that concept. Rather, does this term suggest IEUE (YHWH) in the causal creative activity as originator and controller of cosmic forces, and suggests dynamic rather than temporal references? Furthermore, what Isaiah seems to express is the concept of IEUE (YHWH) as transcending that of creation; he retorts to circulocutionary phrases like "I am the First and I am the Last" (Isah 41:4; 48:12). What is quite apparent for the casual reader is that if Isaiah wished to express the eternity of God, all that would have been required would have been to say that IEUE (YHWH) had no beginning and would have no ending. At the same time we recognize that the human cognitive disposition cannot compass the infinite, and this is present as the Hebrews Scriptures writers wisely refrain from attempting the impossible. Nor does there appear to be any text in the Hebrew Scriptures where *olam* is mentioned to convey an ending; this notion has prob-

---

15. Barton and Muddiman, *Oxford Bible Commentary,* 467.

ably been anachronistically associated with the word by writers influence by later philosophy. To be sure, we can argue that the life of God when expressed by the word *olam* in the absolute sense means eternal; we cannot deny this, and furthermore we could argue that is the correct sense when speaking of God as being the eternal God. This is to some degree true, yet we can further argue, since this is the case that *olam* and its plural form *olamin* in every which way denotes eternal, it could not refer to a limited duration of time and that when using superlative *olam* and *olam*, the translation into English as "for ever and ever" is indeed correct.

However, such a hypothesis goes against the grain of biblical hermeneutics; we seek to understand the sacred Scripture through the prisms of sound interpretation of the biblical text. We can argue that this is not a hermeneutic of suspicion, which is the international fallacy of presenting a hypothesis based on a dispensational bent of one's disposition. This, however, is not the case, as the argument for clarity of the text comes in view when engaging with the Hebrew grammar; we take into consideration the nuances and the grammatical construct of the Hebrew syntax, thereby giving a rendering that is close to the inspired original. This may be so, but one cannot get away from the fact that the word "eternal" means just that. Take the Psalms, for instance. There are retributive Psalms within the psalter. These texts are in themselves proof texts that the wicked will be cut off forever.[16] Many of these retributive Psalms must be felt according to the context in which they are read. Such terms like "cut off," "removed," "destroyed," and so on, are in fact expressions of the psalmist, and the thinking of the original writer and his first reader. To make these Psalms apply to an eschatological judgment is again a hermeneutic fallacy, and goes against the grain of appropriate interpretation of text.

Nevertheless, the eternal separation in the Psalms argues that the wicked will be separated forever, and that they will not see the face of God. This again is mixed metaphors, as we seek to correlate anthropomorphic ideas with inanimate objects by syntactically linking it with judgment. Is this not a fair approach to interpretation of Scripture as we look at the judgment text of the Hebrew First Testament? "*Yet IEUE-Adonai (YHWH), shall sit enthroned for the eon; He will establish His throne for judgment, And He shall judge the habitant with justice; He shall adjudicate the national groups with equity.*" (Ps 9:7–8, CVOT). If he reigns forever and not for the eon, we can argue, when will he not reign, and will he not make redress to all

---

16. Ps 37:20, 68:2, 106:18, and 145:20.

social groups on the earth, and will he not correct and right the wrongs of the poor and the oppressed? Will that be a continuance of judgment, will that judgment start and last for a specific period of time? Note the text; the truth is rather obscure in most of our popular versions. His throne is established for judgment, that is, his throne is set up a specific purpose; the problem with the notion of judgment is that within Western thinking, it is construed as synonymous for punishment. However, in this text this is not the case; he will adjudicate the national groups with equity. The NIV reads "*He will govern his peoples with justice.*" The problem with the structure of the sentence in the NIV is that it does not appear that God will dole out justice to all national groups on the earth. Furthermore, the most popular of the Reformed theological Bibles, the ESV (English Standard Version), makes a vast improvement over the NIV: "*and he judges the world with righteousness . . .*" There is no indication of punishment in the text, but only the act of setting right wrongs. His throne is established or set up to set right the wrongs of humanity, by redressing the wrongs. This is confirmed in Psalm 72:2: "*May he adjudicate your people with righteousness, and Your humbled ones with redress.*" All of these correlating texts seem to address the notion that God in His divine judgment exercises rightness and it is not synonymous with punishment. God judges based on His character; "*Judge me according to your righteousness*" (Ps 35:24). What is indicative of this text is the notion that the psalmist was able to understand the nature of God, and in so doing redress the wrongs of humanity. Therefore, judgment could not be everlasting, as it would take into consideration the definitive idea of what everlasting is. If everlasting has no beginning or ending by definition and God is eternal because he has no beginning and no ending, then how is there an eternal judgment? Judgment must have a beginning and a conclusion, and therefore it could not be eternal. However, some scholars would argue that the metaphor of judgment is speaking of God's attributes, such as his majesty and greatness, along with punishment. Arius the second-century church father argued that the God of the Old Testament is not to be worshiped because He was different from the God of the New. The Old Testament God appears to be a narcissistic bully, spoilt at best. Thus Arius embraced the "New" over the "Old," and this called for drastic moves for the canonization of both testaments under the auspices of Athanasius in the fourth century. We cannot simply argue that judgment is eternal, just as much as we cannot argue that the lives of human beings are eternal. To be sure, when taking into consideration the death of Adam in the primeval creation of the pre-antediluvian world, did God mean that Adam should live forever? Was there a mistake on the part of the Divine? There is no suggestion in the text to think that.

Furthermore, the life of men and women were considered to be a lot longer than what we have today. What were the reasons for this? Did God intend to annihilate humanity in the flood by only saving eight souls? Will those people be resurrected for judgment, or are they already judged? These questions are not unanswerable; they would, however, require more analysis of the argument and critical discussion of the issues at hand. Hence, we are unable to make definitive judgment on texts that would suggest otherwise. The matter in consideration is the Hebrew word *olam* and its antecedent. From the deductive arguments stated, Olam is obscure, hidden; it refers to that which is beyond horizon, it was not considered as everlasting. The Hebrews spoke little of an event or situation that was beyond their horizon, they knew little about the where and how of life beyond the Sheol. Later as we have seen in the Second Temple Period, Israel had developed sophisticated ideas that were borrowed from their former masters like the Persians, Babylonians, and Greeks. Such ideas of immortality like souls, the afterlife, and free will were developed, and of course were demonstrated in the writings of Jewish thought. This is clearly exhibited in the poetic prose of the books by post-exilic prophets. Furthermore we argued that *olam, olamin* and *olam-avad* (which means to the future until) has nothing to do with eternal; by default when speaking of the life of God, we speak of the God of the eons. Not that he is not eternal, that is an absolute fact, and we could say that *olam* could mean eternal in the text when referring to the deity; but as we look at the context when this word is employed in relation to the Deity, we will see that it is not referring to the life of God, but his divine activities during the *eonian* times. The stated fact is that God made the eons (Heb 1:2). Thus, when we speak of God as the God of the eons, we mean that he is the Father and the owner of time itself; we are not inferring that God is confined or limited to the eons of time, nor should we limit him as such. What we are inferring is that God is the God of the eons; He made it, thus it,is he who owns it and regulates it, therefore he is the God of time because he made time and in this case he made the eons. He plans and disposes what he will during its course.

What we sought to do is to argue that the word *olam* in the First Testament is in fact limited to time. We supplied the rationale for the word *olam* by highlighting key text, not in their totality, but we sought to engage with the Greek LXX and the Hebrew variant, demonstrating the nuance of the language. Furthermore, we tabulated the argument that context determines the meaning of the text. Thus, we sought to do justice to the text by providing appropriate investigation, presenting the evidence concerning this Hebrew word *olam*.

We will continue this investigation by looking at the Greek in the Second or New Testament. We will analyze the book *Terms For Eternity* by Ramelli and Konstan in a dialectical approach, by asking if the word eon relates to timelessness, or is it limited to a duration of time. We will investigate how the word *aion* is used during the intertestamental period and its emphasis on the Greek Scriptures. We will begin by looking at how the Greek text appears contradictory on the surface of it. Furthermore, we will refer to the New Testament or Second Testament as the Greek Scriptures. What we seek to do is present an argument that will provide a soteriological approach to how the entire salvific history is played out during the course of the eons.

The entire whigmaleerie of the teaching of the eons is not something that is conjured by some sort of doctrinaire that has no relevance too salvation. On the contrary, we will contend that the entire basis of salvation hinges on this single doctrine itself. Furthermore, we will highlight key facts from the Greek from reputable New Testament scholars as to what this word means in the Greek. Does it reflect eternity, or a limited duration? By looking into the etymological usage, we can deduce that the signifier *aion* is in fact a scriptural word and that the use of *aion* is not endless in its duration.

9

Aion αἰών ἀίδις

THE GREEK WORD ΑΙΩΝΩΝ is a strange word, Barclay contends, as it has three meanings.[1] Plato took the word *aiōnios*—he may have coined it—and gave it special mysterious meaning. Plato employed it to denote something that has neither beginning nor end, is subject to neither, that which is above time, but of which time is a moving image.[2] Ramelli and Konstan noted that there were two words that denoted "eternal," that is *aiônios* (αἰώνιος) and *aïdios* (ἀίδις), and translated to the Latin *aeternus*. The first is derived from the word *aion*, which may signify a lifetime or a long temporal period (an eon). The second adjective is derivative from the adverb *aiea* (always).[3] Clearly, Ramilli and Konstan do not agree with Barclay's view that this word originated with Plato, nor do they see this word in a trifold sense, but in a dichotomic sense. Furthermore, unlike Barclay who sees this word *aiôn* rooted in Greek philosophy, Ramilli and Konstan posit that there is no evidence in the Homer classics, it may have had some mystical usage. This is what Barclay suggests; however, the *adjective* aiônios, and

---

1. Life time. Herodotus speaks of ending our *aiōn*, an age, a generation, or an epoch. The Greeks speaks of this present *aiōn* and of the *aiōn* which is to come as a very long space of time. The prepositional phrase *apaiōnos* means from old. Barclay, *Daily Study Bible*, 33.

2. Barclay, *Daily Study Bible*, 34.

3. While there is often a considerable overlap in the employment of the two Greek words, they however possess two distinct semantic trajectories, and contrivances and divergences in their meaning correspond. Ramelli and Konstan, *Terms For Eternity*, 5.

AION αιών άίδις

aïdios express "forever."[4] Barclay did not in any sense of the word argue that Plato meant that the word meant indefinite continuance. Both adjectives, αιώνιος and άίδι, were used by Plato, but out of fifteen occurrences of άίδις only four were discovered in the pseudo-Platonic *Definitions,* and two in the *Axiochus,* dubiously attributed to Plato. Consequently, *áidion* is defined as *"that which exists throughout time, and is uncreated and not subject to corruption."*[5] Barclay and Ramelli agree with Konstan that Plato's usage did not express eternity in its original usage. They also agreed that Plato introduced the concept (29 A3, 5) with reference to the pattern that the demiurge used in creating the sensible cosmos by perceiving "to eternity" (πρός το άίδιον). άιων does not unambiguously signify "eternity," Plato used it initially in Greek literature. It is also apparent that the normalized adjective did not express eternity in its own right.[6]

The Creator made a decision to make a moving image of eternity. The Creator was glad when he saw his universe, and he wished to make it as nearly like the eternal universe as it could be.[7] Furthermore, *aïdos* and *aiônios* appear to be virtually interchangeable when we consider that the model from the universe is "an eternal living thing" (ζώον άίδιον) and its nature is eternal (τον ζωον ονσα αιώνιος). Both "eternity" (αίωνα) and "eternal-being" (άίδιοζ ουσία) are tense-less, without distinction of time whether past, present, or future.[8] From these deductive statements from the classics, we note that the notion of *aion* coined by Plato for the *Republic* did not express an endless duration.

---

4. In the Homeric hymn, the gods are said to have a "permanent seat" (έδρην άίδιον έλαχες) in all the dwellings of gods and mortals, an expression that does not necessarily imply a technical sense of "eternal." Ramelli and Konstan, *Terms For Eternity,* 7.

5. In the *Republic* (363 D2), Plato employed the adjective in connection with drunkenness (υέθην αιωνιον), where it bears the notion of "continuous" consistent with the traditional sense of αιώνιος, the latter meaning "unregenerated" as well; the human body and soul have beginning but no end, according to Plato, whereas God has neither beginning nor end. Ramelli and Konstan, *Terms For Eternity,* 12–13.

6. Ramelli and Konstan, *Terms For Eternity,* 13.

7. Barclay, *Daily Study Bible,* 34; Ramelli and Konstan, *Terms For Eternity,* 12.

8. And yet Plato appeared to have discovered the term *ion as* a special designation for his whigmaleerie of eternity as timeless, one that could substitute for the nominal phrase *to audio,* and with the new sense of *aio, aiônios* too seems to have come into its own as a signifier of what is beyond time. Ramelli and Konstan, *Terms For Eternity,* 14.

Doctrine of the Eons

Barclay, Ramelli, and Konstan highlight a salient point. In their view, they suggest that the term "time" itself refers to the Deity as opposed to humanity, thus it can only apply to the life of the deity.[9] This argument is essentially faulty, as it implies that human beings are not given *aionan* life, and that *aionan* life is exclusive to Deity, and could convey the notion of timeless eternity, when in fact we would not be able to apply this to soteriology. Furthermore, if the *aion* could not be equated to the life of mankind on the earth, we then would ask, what would be the best term to define life for Christians? Barclay fails to apply *aion* to the life of humanity as promised in the escalation in the Greek Scriptures.[10] Yet, from the statements mentioned, the *aions* in relation to God in the absolute sense is eternal, because God himself is perfect; he is timeless [ἀειτελής τουτεστιν ἀεί τέλειος], and absolutely perfect in every respect [παντελής τουτέστι πάντη τέλειος]. The notion of *aion* in the thinking of Plato was not anthropomorphic; this was seen later in Christian writings, and furthermore, life and the duration of life was often seen in the idea of the soul, which was reflected later in early patristical thought.

Furthermore, the notion among the second-century BCE philosophers clearly exhibited the idea of αἰώνιος and ἀίδις as perpetual, going on to eternity. The former indicates an eternity beyond time, whereas the latter is also used for an infinite continuity in time, whether in the past or the future.[11] In relation to the student of twenty years, Aristotle, in his *Metaphysics*, when making a contrast between the usage of the αἰώνιος and ἀίδις, was not altogether clear as to how eternity is equated with the usage of these two words. Furthermore, Aristotle was not one of those who employed this term in the absolute sense. The term was equated with "un-generated," (αγεντων) and 46 eternal occurrences of "eternal" (ἀίδια) are incorporeal, "always the same time in the same disposition."[12] Consequently, in the *Life*

---

9. "The essence of the word *aionios* is that it's the word of the eternal order as contrasted with the order of the world; it is the word of Deity as contrasted with humanity; essentially it is the word which can be properly applied to no other than God." Barclay, *Daily Study Bible*, 35.

10. "The middle of the Platonist Acinus, at *Didascalicus* 9.2, refers to the Platonic definition of the Ideas with the term αἰώνιος, in reference as the eternal thoughts of God," [παραδειγμα αἰωνίους] of entities in nature, and he offers definition of αἰώνιος in reference to God's ideas are eternally conceived by God." Ramelli and Konstan, *Terms For Eternity*, 17.

11. Ramelli and Konstan, *Terms For Eternity*, 21.

12. [κατά ταύτα και ωσαυτως εχόντων] "In On Abstinence 4.10.20, the gods are αιδιοι, and in On the cave of the Nymphs 33, the providence of intellectual nature (νοερά φύσις),

of Pythagoras, ἀίδις, the metaphysical incorporated Platonic idea of αἰώνιος suggested an eternity lofter than time and peculiarity of intelligible entities. In an anthropomorphic sense, the intellectual soul is an entity which is reconciled with the intellect in the αἰών.[13] Through these statements from ancient Greek philosophy, what we sought to do is show the diverse views in relation to this term (*aion*) αιών. We sought to engage the thought of how this word is employed in the late second century BCE, though it may not in itself be a comprehensive overview of the prevailing views that were current during that era. More details are from the work *Terms For Eternity*. What is clearly elucidated from this periscope, is that the words ἀίδις and αἰώνιος were employed interchangeably as dialogue in relations to human dignitaries and in the diverse writings. Thus, the definition of this word and its development during this period clearly demonstrated that there was no apparent link with αἰών and its Hebrew equivalent. Clearly this goes to show that Hebrew as a Semitic language would have been lost during the time of the Greek empire. We then ask could αἰών be perceived as a perpetual motion going on to eternity? How we understand this interim of human beings is not altogether clear, yet we do understand—from the writing of Plato and others during that period—that the soul was considered immortal and intellectual, and much of this was developed in later Christian thought. How then does Plato equate eternity with αἰών? This is something of debate with philosophers, up to this current time. What the αἰών is in the life to come is still a matter of philosophical debate that Plato articulated in the *Republic*; he highlighted some of the significant points in which this word is employed. Furthermore, in what way did Barclay think that the word *aion* meant eternal? He gave three different definitions, yet he felt that the word expressed some timeless eternity of some sort. He clearly elucidated that the term used by Plato did in fact demonstrate that the signifier in the original language expressed limitless duration; how long was this duration, he did not specify, but he clearly agreed with Plato that this word did speak of the life of God in the absolute sense. From what he equates as eternal, Ramelli and Konstan sought on the other hand to provide a workable praxis of how this word was used among the classics. They sought to bring to the attention of the reader key aspects of how αἰών and ἀίδις were employed within the prism of the third and second century BCE. They also highlighted key aspects of how this word was used in every-

---

which governs the universe, is ἀίδιοζ, and is also called αειθαληζ, "ever-flourishing."'" Ramelli and Konstan, *Terms For Eternity*, 22.

13. Ramelli and Konstan, *Terms For Eternity*, 23.

day usage. Clearly much of what was expressed was limited in an absolute sense, as eternity is always viewed as the life of God. What wasn't clear from them is how Plato used this term in relation to the soul—regarding Plato's rational soul, pro-soul, or bar soul, we do not have the specifics. Nor do Ramelli and Konstan clarify this; regardless, the specific purpose that they set out to do was accomplished in setting the tone for our attention to turn to the Hebrew and LXX Greek Scriptures and then to the New Testament Greek Scriptures, looking at every occurrence where this word is employed. We will tabulate how this word was used during the Second Temple Period, demonstrating that over a period of time certain doctrines and practices, foreign to the Jews, soon became practice and Hellenization became the norm of the day. Thus, Platonic ideas were incorporated into the theological praxis of Jewish thought. The next section will focus on how this word is used in light of late Greek writings of Scriptures.

10

ἄϊδις, αἰών in the Greek Scriptures

BARCLAY ARGUED THAT THIS word was a very difficult word to express in its relation to time.[1] As we parley over these matters, we will attempt to argue that the word aides became discounted with the arrival of the Septuagint around the third and fourth centuries BCE. Furthermore, as Ramelli and Konstan suggest, αἰώνιος with αἰών correspond to their Hebrew antecedent *olâm*.[2] The Greek version of the Old Testament clearly demonstrated that this word corresponded with its Hebrew equivalent, consequently, what we have discovered is that it does not express endless duration in its usage. Also αἰών is construed as remote time, remotest time, perpetual, past, further continuance, days of old, long time past. Barclay's response to Plato with which Ramilli and Konstan agreed, is that when in the absolute sense speaking of the life of God, it referred to eternal.[3] A particular employment

---

1. Barclay, *Daily Study Bible*, 33.

2. "Gen 7:13, 19, the perpetual frequency, along with αἰώνιος, occurs with impressive frequency, it is used as the petal covenant with human beings after the deluge, commented by the rainbow, is termed διαθήκη αἰώνιος, as in Gen 7:13, 19 is that between God and Abraham and his descendants, Ex 3:16 it is the compact between Israel sanctified by the observance of the Sabbath, which in turn called "an "eternal sign" (σημεῖον ἀιώνιον)" (Ramelli and Konstan, *Terms For Eternity*, 37–38).

3. "The uses what have been outlined front terms αἰώνιος and αιων correspond close as we aforementioned to those of the Hebrew olam, in the sense of "hidden time" unknowable, by virtue by being distant past or future, and that anion is never accompanied by an adjective indicating duration, length, or interval of time, as occurred often in secular Greek. On the use of Olam in the plural, in post-exiling books Orban, 108–9, tabulates, for the sense of "eternity," although it is better rendered as "ages" (Barclay, *Daily*

Doctrine of the Eons

of the αἰώνιος is that in reference to the world, the αἰων and the world is synchronized. I agree and will speak of this later.

Furthermore, the terms αἰώνιος and αἰων correspond closely, as has been mentioned, in all ocurrences. In 439 occurrences of *olām*, only eight are translated in some other form. This is highly significant. Note in Psalm 61:5 (60:5) there occurs the form of time as the plural *olāmîm*, translated as εἰς αἰωνας, "for the ages" or "for the eons," and παντων των αἰωνων (*kol-olāmîm*). In Ecclesiastes 1:10, what may seem new is said, nonetheless, to have happened "in eons that were before us" (*lōlāmîm*, ἐν τοίς αιώνιος). In 2 Chronicles 6:2; Solomon constructs a temple "for the eons" (*òlāmîm*, εἰσαι τους αἰωνας). There are a number of other occurrences, both in the Hebrew and the Greek version of the Old Testament, of this word αἰων and its plural form. There were other instances where *ölâm* is rendered as εἰς αἴωνα χρονον, and where αἰων appears to be taken as an improper adjective with χρόνος.[4] We have given special treatment of the word *aion* and its corresponding Hebrew equivalence, clearly demonstrating that this word in the Hebrew Scriptures does not express eternity and that all of its antecedent text does not in any way express endless duration. Nor did the Greek writers in the secular writings express the term αἰώνιος as a term that relates to endless duration; αιών, which is basically an earlier form of our word *aeon*, is construed as we are aware, for an age, an epoch, or a period of time that is in some way, from some point of view, a rounded whole, complete in itself.[5]

Furthermore, as we have engaged with Rameilli and Konstan's *Terms for Eternity*, which explored the Greek version of the Old Testament called the Septuagint, we have noted that the term *olam* and *aion* in their purest form do not express eternity, nor did the signifier *olam* and its Greek equivalent express such in the ancient lexicons. However, in relating to the Greek vocabulary, its adjective form άίδις in contrast with αἰωνας belongs to the philosophical lexicon and signifies "eternal" in the strictest sense; it occurs only twice as we have highlighted, which we found in the apocryphal

---

Study Bible, 41).

4. "Again *lôlâm*, generally translated by εἰς τον αιώνα, is translated with the preposition, at Ezek 43:7,9, Zach 1:5, where it is mentioned that the prophets will not live τον αἰωνα; Prov 10:30, Eccl 1:4. God's Kingdom is rendered by what appears to be a genitive of time, τού αιώνος" (Ramelli and Konstan, *Terms For Eternity*, 43–44).

5. "Hence we mean speak of aeons, or ages, which must have been consumed by the geological changes of the earth, and of the still vaster aeons, or ages, necessary for the great astronomical changes that must have preceded the periods during which the void earth was taking its present form" (Cox, *Salvator Mundi*, 101).

writings (the Greek version of the Old Testament). The problem that we have encountered, as Ramilli and Kostan highlighted, was that the two words in themselves had in some texts different denotations. As far as we are aware, following the interpretive principles in the context determines the meaning of the text, therefore this is necessary in order to translate this word accordingly and to harness an appropriate understanding of these two words. Poulliot further showed the fact that "*aidios as being eternal or everlasting, that this word could not express endless in its original form.*"[6]

Cox, in his work *Salvator Mundi*, suggests that the word "eternal" and its antecedent "everlasting" are employed at will, that is, there is little if any attention given as to what this word really meant in its original form.[7] Cox further argues that "eternal denotes above and beyond time, that which is independent of duration; that which you no more calculate on the sequences of time than you can weigh music by the pound or measure beauty with a foot-rule. "Eternal" transcends standards and limits of time, that which above and beyond, before and after, that which encompasses as well as penetrates and suffuses it, is clearly the greater and nobler of the two."[8] Even Cox agrees that when the word eternal is used in the absolute sense it refers to God.

Consequently, it cannot be denied that there are elements of enduring punishment which we cannot deny, yet it appears that such occurrences definitely express a limited duration; in relation to humans, it could not

---

6. "The fact is that Jesus never used this word; if He had used it, however, *adios* appears in the Greek text only two times: Rom 1:20 and Jude 6. Surpassingly, Scripture never associates *adios*, which is an adjective, with life. In the Greek, it never reads *aidos zoe* (life); instead, it always reads *aiōnios zoe,* a phrase used 41 times in the Greek Scripture, again depending on the translation. If *adios* were joined with *zoe* (life) throughout the Greek text, then we would have no argument, and would have to agree with all who hold to eternal life based on accepted definition of the word eternal. The fact that it not joined with life is a strong indicator that something else meant, and it behooves us to discover what this is" (Poulliot, "Article#57: Eternal or Eonian?," 3).

7. "The word "eternal" bears two great meanings, and is used in two different senses. Popularly and loosely it is used to denote that which last for ever; but as it used by many of most eminent thinkers and theologians, instead of denoting that which endures through that the successions of time" (Cox, *Salvator Mundi*, 97).

8. ""Eternal" and "everlasting" should be treated as synonymous. This indicates that which continues through the whole of duration; other, that which is out of duration and above it, of which the measures and sequences of time are necessary part. This done expresses quantity, the other quality. "Everlasting" denotes that which last for ever; "eternal," that which is scriptural ad divine" (Cox, *Salvator Mundi*, 98).

Doctrine of the Eons

be construed as endless duration.⁹ Thus we can see further evidence from the Greek Scriptures, commonly called the New Testament. We will revisit some of the statements echoed by Jesus and his usage of the term, as we have already mentioned. This does not go without saying that the Greek and the Hebrew equivalent demonstrates that the word did not express eternity. As this cannot be overstated, during the period of the Greek empire under Alexander the Great, through the writing of Plato and others, in their usage of the word, the word did not express in secular form "eternity" in any sort of way. As aforesaid, the classics and the reading of this word άίδις became disused, replaced by the word αίωνας which became the lingua franca in the writing of the classics. However, Heleen Keizer posits the difficulty in finding the word among the classic and in Hellenistic literature.¹⁰ She also argued concerning the difficulty in tracing the origin of the word.¹¹ Fragments of early Hellenistic poets were discovered in the third century in a similar vein to Homer, like the tragedy of Moschion.¹²

The occurrence of αίωνας, when speaking in the strictest sense, spoke of the life of God. When speaking in terms of the life of humanity, it was considered temporal and did not reflect endless eternity at any given time. Also, in relation to retributive punishment as endless punishment, it only expressed a temporal punishment; Ramelli and Konstan also noted that the word αίωνας could not speak of endless eternity in any shape or form.¹³ The ground covered in this aspect was to highlight this term as exhibited in the classics, much of which is covered in indepth detail in *Terms For Eternity*

---

9. "As we have noted Origen, just as many other Christians writers, observes the same distinction as the one apparently intimated in 4 Macc applying to the future life either αίωνας, or άίδις, while for death win the future employs only αίωνας and never άίδις" (Cox, *Salvator Mundi*, 50).

10. "Among the 13 occurrences of aiōn in Homer pics (8th century BCE) the only instance of the word construed with a preposition. Centuries later, in the Hellenistic period, the phrase *apaiōons is used* in the Septuagint as a fixed expression having the sense of "from time immemorial"" (Keizer, *Life Time Entirety*, 17).

11. It is easy to race the use and meaning of *aiōn* in the third, second and first century BCE, (Keizer, *Life Time Entirety*, 47).

12. ανερ από αίωος ωλένιου και με χηρην λειπιζ my husband from aiōn you were cut off young and leave me widowed behind" (Keizer, *Life Time Entirety*, 17).

13. "Virtually all of the expressions with αίωνας in the Septuagint have behind them *alum* and for αίωνας, the sense of "eternal" to the extent that tit present, derives only from association God, and this, all in all, relatively rarely. Otherwise, we have a multiplicity of other senses, among which the laters topper, chronologically speaking, speaking, appears to partake of the eschatological significance that it will acquire in the New Testament and in the Christian Fathers" (Keizer, *Life Time Entirety*, 48).

ἀίδις, αἰών IN THE GREEK SCRIPTURES

which provides tangible evidence that this is the case. There were other notable works, such as the thoughts echoed by C.F Keizer's work "Time and Eternity," which argued that infinity is not an intrinsic or necessary connotation of *aiōn*, either in the Greek or the biblical usage (*ôlâm*), or the Aramaic equivalent (*alam*).[14] Gladstone further posits the notion of eternity by translating the Greek εις τον αιώνα, εις τούς αιώνας, έως αιώνιος, εις των αιώνων. Although he did not categorically state that this word expressed eternity,[15] he conflated the Hebrew and Greek word but misunderstood the point, thereby giving a rendering obscured from Scripture.

This section sought to engage our thinking as to how the Greek version (LXX) was seen in light of the word *aiōn*. Thereby, providing the framework that this very same word discovered in the Greek corresponded with the Hebrew equivalent, *olām*, we discussed that this word did not express endless eternity in the strictest sense; however, when it did speak as such, it only spoke in the strictest sense in relation to God. In relation to humanity, it is employed metaphorically, not in a literal sense, to "time" or "limited duration." The Hebrews did not have a word to express endless eternity, nor was that usage employed in the Hebrew Scriptures as such. The idea of endlessness was not in the vocabulary of the Hebrew people, as they had no idea of an endless eternity. It was not until the Second Temple Period that those new ideas of endlessness, free will, iImmortality of the soul, and so on, appeared. These were developed through the writings of the Persians, Babylonians, and Greeks. We presented this idea in this chapter. We engaged with *Terms For Eternity* and other important works. This leads us to pursue further in our engagement of the word as it was employed in the Greek New Testament. We will investigate some of the most important texts used in the synoptic tradition, as well as other seemingly eschatological and soteriological texts, that may appear to suggest otherwise.

---

14. Girdlestone, *Synonyms of the Old Testament*, 48.

15. "Some translators have rendered these passages literally and without respect to their usage in the LXX (e.g. "Unto the ages of the ages and so on) In 1 Tim 1:17, God is called King of the ages (AV King Eternal); whiles in Heb 1:2, 11. 3 He said 'he made the ages' (AV worlds). The rendering of the AV is no doubt right in the first case, and probably in the second also. Ages and worlds bear relation to one another as time and space do, and the process of creating worlds was means of bringing ages into being" (Girdlestone, *Synonyms of the Old Testament*, 318).

Doctrine of the Eons

The New Testament serves as the pancreas of biblical theology, it exhibits some of the most profound text when speaking of life and the life to come. As we continue in this chapter, we will highlight some of the key texts in the synoptic tradition and Pauline corpus.

Matthew 21:19

και ιδών συκην επίθεση οδου ηλυτην και ουδέν εύπεπτα έν αυτη ΕΙ υή φύλλα μόνον, και λέγει αυτή, Μηκέτι έκανε σου καρπός γενηται εις τον αιωνα.

And seeing the fig tree by the way side he went it, and found nothing on it but leaves only. And said he said to it "May no fruit ever come from you again" (RSV).

From the above statement we can deduce that the word αιωνα in this context did not express forever as our modern translations express it. Jesus, seeing that the fig produced leaves yet no fruit, serves it as a dating parable of the nation of Israel, for the eon—that is, the *eis*, in the Greek "into" or "for," so it expresses the negative "not." This seems to suggest that in this current eon the nation of Israel was doomed, for it was unable to produce fruits for repentance during the initial inaugural ministry of Jesus; this is the thought expressed by A.E Knoch[16] and is also agreed with by Bengel.[17] This is the judgment of the nation of Israel, that they will not produce fruit for the eon, but not forever—such is the thought that Jesus sought to express.

---

16. "The fig, the olive, and the vine present varied views of the kingdom. Perhaps we should include the bramble as Jotham did in this parable (Jud 9:8–15) The bramble is that false flare of authority exercised by Babylon the Great which has a kingdom over the Kings of the earth (Rev.17:18. The Vine speaks of that which cheers the heart of God and man. Then will be joy. The olive speak of light. The fig brings sweetness. It is the national in scope, and it is in contrast with Rome, represented as the wild fig tree (Lk 17:6)Israel doom is sealed. It is like a fig tree with leaves but no fruit. The fig forms some of its fruits before its leaves, unless it's barren. This fig tree had evidently anticipated the eon and put forth its leaves very early. So were Israel's national pretensions. They made a beautiful show of national righteousness, but there was no genuine reality to their claims" (Knoch, *Concordant Commentary*, 4).

17. "Therefore the fruit it should no longer receive sap in vain. Such was the punishment of the Jews" (Bengel, *New Testament Commentary*, 248).

ἀίδις, αἰών IN THE GREEK SCRIPTURES

John 6:51

Εγώ είμαι ὁ ἄρτος ὁ ζωάρ του ουρανού καταβας εάν φάγη έκ τούτου του άρτου ζήσει τον αιώνα, και ότι άρτος δε ὁν εγώ δώσω η σάριξ μυιν εστιν υπέρ του κόσμου ζωής.

"I am the living Bread which comes down from heaven; if any ones eat of this bread, he will live [αἰώνα-eons] forever, and the bread of life is my flesh."

This is one of the of the seven of the "I am" sayings within Johannine literature; Jesus employs the ego and the metaphor that he is the bread and that by partaking of him we would live forever as the traditional translation of the text suggests. Yet this is not the case as far as we are aware: Western and patristical thought sought to make this text apply to the Eucharist, but this machination of the flesh of Christ is not what is implied. To live forever because of the bread is not the thought here, as many of the first readers would not have understood the metaphor implied in the text. What this text suggests is commonly called the hard sayings of the Greek Scriptures. The allusion to this text refers not to the time span which Jesus speaks of, life. Knoch suggests that this life is again in the future, and it is that life which is really called "everlasting."[18] Furthermore, the idea of eating of the flesh is appropriation of the life of Christ. This text could refer to or allude to some never-ending life, but the idea of sustaining life in Christ in this vein is as this αἰώνος text suggests. We purpose to illustrate and clearly demonstrate the highly-structured usage of this word in its original form.

John 8:35

ὅτι δε δούλος ούτε μένει εν τη οικία εις τον αιώνα ὁ υιος μένει εις τον αιώνα

Ho dedoulous ou menei en te oikia eis ton *aiōna* [which is a *noun accusative singular masculine*]

ho huios meni eis ton *aiōn* [*noun singular masculine*]

"Slaves do not remain in the house forever; the son does" [traditional rendering].

If this is the case what happens when the son dies? The life of the slave is of the same length as the life of the son. The duration is clearly exhibited

---

18. "As this life has a definite beginning it also has an end. But as the end doe not not come until death is abolished, it changes from *"eonian"* life into actual never-ending life. This will be the portion to all" (Knoch, *Concordant Commentary,* 150).

in this text as limited for the eon (age) and could not extend beyond that. So to suggest an endless life in the text, one would then have to ask how long is an eon in this passage? The answer is not far to seek. It is as long as they live. To eisegetically read this particular text in the light of endless life would cause a series of interpretational damage to the authorial intent of the text.

Hebrews 5:6

Κανχς και ετερω λέει λέγει Συ του αιώνα κατά την ταζιν Μελχισεδεκ,
    katas legei kai en heater sy hiereus eis ton aiōna [*noun Accusative singular masculine*] kata ten taxin Melchizedek.

The text here in Hebrews speaks of a number of things initially that the writer purports to demonstrate: that the priesthood had failed, that there was a far superior priesthood that had been replaced by Christ, and that this was a superior priesthood. Note that the αιώνα again is the noun accusative singular masculine which suggests that, like adjectives and nouns in English, the action is acted upon the subject; the subject is a better priesthood. The "you" is a plural pronoun of the second person, in this case speaking of Christ, who is of the priesthood of Melchizedek, but this priesthood is not forever. For elsewhere in Scripture we have a subjection of Christ, such as in the Pauline corpus, borrowing from an ancient Christian hymn sung in the second century.[19] Furthermore we have the new heavens and earth, this then demonstrates that the mediatoral role of Christ could not last forever, based on the subjection, i.e., an annulment and dethronement of death.[20] From this *eis aiōnios*, we have 10 percent of our New Testament usage of this term. Glelesnoff pointed out the absurdity of employing this word as a signifier for eternity.[21] The divergent employment of this word that occurs in the Greek Scriptures New Testament is 129 times; the noun occurs 128 times and the adjective 71 times.[22]

---

19. Phil 2:10–11: "that at the name of Jesus every knee should bow, in heaven and earth and under the earth, and every tongue confess that Jesus Christ is Lord to the Glory of God the Father" (RSV).

20. 1 Cor 15:28.

21. "It remains to point out that the Ages or Aeons are neither synonymous nor co-eval with "Eternity"" (Hanson, *Greek Word Aion-Aionios*, 17).

22. "Recent translation rendered the noun seventy-two times ever, twice, eternal, thirty-six time world, seven times never, three times evermore, twice world, twice ages, once course, once world without end and twice worlds, twenty-five times everlasting, and once former ages" (Hanson, *Greek Word Aion-Aionios*, 42).

Jude 13

κύματα ἄγρια θάλασσας επαφοζοντα τας εαυτών αισχύνης πλανάται οίς ὁ ζόφος του σκότους εις αιώνα τετήρηται.

From the above text we can deduce Madristic rabbinical teaching coming from the Lord Jesus Christ's brother, who borrows from the ancient rabbinical writings. Was Jude teaching everlasting punishment as he alluded to the metaphors of sea, trees, waves, and stars? The notion of false teaching appears to be the subject of the text. Beale and Carson think this is the case;[23] the context does not reflect endlessness, nor was it the authorial intent of the author to express endlessness in the text. The *aiōna* (noun accusative singular masculine) in this text is preceded by *eis*, which is a preposition, thus "into the eons will they be judged." This text no way infers otherwise.

However, another text in Jude seems to suggest otherwise: ώζ Σόδομα και Γόμορρα και Άι Παρί αυτας πόλεις τον ομοιον τροπον τούτος εκπόρνευσαι και απελθούσαι οπισω σαρκός ετέρας πρόκειται δείγμα πυρός αιωωιου [*adjective genitive singular nuter*] δικην υπεχουσαι. "Wild waves of the sea, cast ring up the foam of their own shame; wandering stars for whom the neither gloom of darkness has been reserved for ever" (RSV).

"As Sodom and Gomorrah and the cites about them in like manner to theses committing ultra-prostitution, and coming away after their flesh, are lying before us a specimen of the justice of fire (*eonian*)" (my translation).[24] The adjective form of the word αιωωιου is thus relating to the common translation of everlasting punishment on the wicked. This is the popular teaching among Western theologians. Yet does this text teach as such? The genitive of *aiōnian* is followed by an additional noun genitive singular neuter in the word (fire). Thus, in our quest for clarification of this text, the imagery

---

23. "Jude develops his series of Metaphors from four shares of nature land (tree), air (clouds), swear, and heaven (starts), he draws parallels from the four shares from the writings of 1 Enoch 80. Here we have reached their metaphor:the false teachers are "wild waves of the sea forming up their shame," possibly an echo of Isa 57:20" (Carson and Beale, *Commentary on the New Testament*, 1077).

24. "Just as Sodom and Gomorrah and the surrounding cites, which likewise indulged in sexual immorality and pursued ethical desire, serve as an example by undergoing a punishment of eternal fire" (ESV).

presents a picture, alluding to the judgment (Gen 19:25, 29); furthermore, we have a clear idea from the language of the text that Jude is not alluding to the same conscious eternal torment, which is what leading biblical proponents would advocate.

Because of this, we are to bear in mind that many biblical scholars retained a Latin approach to interpreting this word.[25] How then did the Latin *aeternum* and the Greek *aiōnian*, which both originally referred to the math with "Ionian," come to signify "eternal" in the modern sense? There is no doubt that these words have been made to express what is eternal, the instrument in every case being theology.[26] Furthermore Muller's *Dictionary of Latin and Greek Theological Terms* notes that word did not express eternity in the Latin but was in fact equivalent to the Greek usage.[27]

The condition *sine qua non* of both the Latin and Greek equivalent demonstrates that this did not express endless duration or eternity of some sort, but in fact only demonstrated a limited duration. As an age, that is, *aiōnios* and its Latin variant *seculum*, did not express the current English word found in biblical translations as eternal, everlasting, and forever, but it was limited to an age, and it did not express endless. Consequently, as we resist some of our favorite texts within the synoptic tradition and in Johannine tradition, we will note that this word was used in relation to the life of God as being eternal; as aforesaid in its absolute sense this is the case. Nevertheless, we still have to contend with other alleged problematic biblical text like those found within Pauline corpus, where the writer speaks of this word in relation to salvation and to the lives of humans as well.

---

25. "fluctus feri maris desquamantes suas confusiones, sider errant, quibus procella tenebrarum in aeternum seta est" (*Nestle-Aland Novum Testamentum Latine*, 630).

26. "*aeternum* in the same sense as the Greek αιωωιου, as meaning eonian. Thus Cicero, who died in 43 BCE says of the future, "springtime will be *aeternum*" that is, enduring, ionian. At present springtime is bread, fleeting, seasonal. He was referring to a spring is brief, fleeting, seasonal. He was referring to a sling which will endure. He also refers to God by the same term, as the enduring One" (Thomson, *Whence Eternity*, 20).

27. "Seculum: age or era; the Latin equivalent of αιώνα: Consummatio saculi: *Consummation off the age*; the Latin equivalent of συντέλεια τού αἰωνος i.e., the end of the world. consisting in the destruction of the sinful old word by fire and the creation or recreation of the world in the new age, thus often, *Consummatio humus saeculi* consummation of the age, indicating the beginning of the next age or *seaculum*" (Muller, *Dictionary of Latin and Greek Theological Terms*, 81, 269).

Luke 1:33

Και βασιλεύ δει επί τον οίκον ΙΑκωβ εις τους αιώνας και της Βασίλειος αυτού ουκ εσται τέλος

"And he will reign over the house of Jacob forever" (RSV).

The Latin reads: "et regnant super donut Jacob in aeternum, et regi eius non erit finis."

Was the reign of the new incarnated Christ to occur during his inaugural ministry of three years? Why was it not realized? This question has conjured up a number of trajectories. Israel rejects the Messiah and his kingship, and the time for this was suspended until a future time. The αιώνας is in the plural form and it does not express endlessness but a future time in the eschatological renaissance. New Testament writers would contend otherwise. However we still have to ask ourselves, was the original language of Luke in Greek and its Latin derivative? Muller offers a rendering of *aeternum*; he equates it with *Dei*, thus in his definition God of eternity. This attribute also demonstrated the idea of continuance (*duratio*) of God without beginning and end, and apart from all succession and change.[28] For this reason, we can now argue the change from the Greek to the Latin equivalent in order to express endless duration within the prism of the biblical text, wherever this word occurs. The problem with the Latin approach is that it says nothing of the life of human beings; furthermore, it speaks only of the life of God; in this vein, we agree when speaking of aeternum in the absolute sense. However, when speaking of salvation we tabulate that this word would not be helpful, because salvation definitely has a beginning and will last only up until it becomes a reality in postmortem eschatological soteriology at the end of this eon—in the future in the kingdom of heaven during the millennial reign of Jesus. Thus we contend that in spite of Erasmus's standardization of the Greek text, we must deal with the theology of the Latin fathers, such as Augustine and others, along with the apparent use of the *seculum* and *aeternum* in their writings and in the employment of the Latin Vulgate, which was the version that helped shape Western theology.

---

28. "Boethius contends that eternity is simultaneous and perfect passion of endless life" (Muller, *Dictionary of Latin and Greek Theological Terms*, 28).

Doctrine of the Eons

John 6:51

εγώ είμαι ο άρτος ο ζων ό εκ του ουρανού καταβας εάν τις φαγη εκ τούτου του άρτου ζήσει εις τον αίωνα, και ο άρτος δε ον εγώ δώσω ή σαρς μου έστιν υπέρ της του κόσμου ζωης

"I am the living bread that came down from heaven. If anyone eats of this bread, he will live forever and the bread that I will give forte the life of this word" (ESV).

Latin: Ego sum pants virus qui de caelo descend. Si quis manducaverit ex hoc pane, vivet in aeternum; panise autem, quem ego dado, caro mea est per mundi vita.

In one of the seven "I am" sayings of John's account, Jesus spoke of the eating of the bread and living forever. Numbers of the early church fathers poorly exegete this text, resulting in some unhappy consequences, such as Christians being accused of masticating the flesh of Christ based upon a misreading of this text. Reading from the memoirs of testimonial history, it is understood metaphorically and allegorically; Jesus spoke of the bread like manna in the wilderness when early Israel was led by a theophany under the theocratic rule of God in the wilderness. Was Jesus speaking of living for a Latin *aeternum*, or for the eons, and in what sense is Jesus the bread that people must feed on and thereby live for the eons? "Now it is evident that the Lord had no thought of a life lasting forever. In the case how could he be *raising him in the last day*? The life here spoke of was bestowed in resurrection. There could no resurrection apart from a previous death. As life has a definite beginning it also has an end. But, the end does not come until death is abolished. It changes from *"eonian"* into actual never-ending life."[29] Beale and Carson contend, "this is speaking spiritually, offering salvation to all so that they can live forever."[30] Yet they do not live forever, or only if by lived we mean as life in the spirit. K. Barrett noted in his comment on this text that the phrase alluded to Old Testament text, which attributes the sovereignty of Deity and, therefore, wisdom to God.[31] We are not denying

---

29. Knoch, *Concordant Commentary*, 158.

30. "Jesus the bread from heaven is taken to a new level. Although the manna was heaven-sent as well nurturing and sustain of life, the argument as well as nurturing and sustaining life" (Carson and Beale, *Commentary on the New Testament*, 450).

31. Like many of the characteristics of Johannine vocabulary, "I am has a complicated background. It recalls passages in ancient literature where the goddess Isis declares her virtues and attributes It is an OT phrase representing the majesty and person of the true God" (Black and Rowley, *Peake's Commentary*, 852).

the authorial intent, as second readers within this promissory text; what we are deliberating over is the mere fact that Jesus spoke of rising up on the last day (54). If those who rise up are dead, as Knoch observed, it heightens the tension in the text. Barrett did not clarify the situation in his comment but heightened the obscurity of the text. Bengel comments, "this participle both increases the weight of his dialogs, and affirms that his is not speaking of ordinary bread."[32] What we have deduced from these statements' evidence is that—in such cases where there is little clarity on the text—we may infer that sound hermeneutic practice must be called to mind. As we have noted, if the person feeds on Jesus who is the methodical bread, it did not in any way represent everlasting life, but in fact sustained life for the eons. This did not mean immortality, nor do we read the sacraments into this text, which is what some scholars have done. Rather in the spiritual sense, feeding on Jesus sustains life that if one dies in the Lord, he will raise them up, based on that relationship that they had with him. J. Martin C. Scott entertains the idea in his view that it is a case of identification with the Bread of Life.[33] We wish not to belabor the point further about this text that may allude to the sacraments as Scott and others suggest. It clearly demonstrates the fact that many New Testament writers overlook this point, and don't see that the point of life (*eonian*) is offered in relation to identifying with Christ.

ΕΙΣ ΤΟΥΣ ΑΙΩΝΑΣ ΤΩΝ ΑΙΩΝΩΝ

This is the same as the Hebrew polytonic superlative adjective. The Latin equivalent of "to the eons of the eons" (ages of the ages) is saecula saeculorum.[34] The Latin derivative is still used as secular, doing things that have no religious connections to it. The Romans used the Greek Aeolian games to make the Saecula games in Athens, Corinth, and such places. Hence this

---

32. "Jesus skillfully framed his words that at the time, and always they would indeed apply literally to the spiritual enjoyment in himself" (Dunn, *Eerdman's Commentary*, 609).

33. "It is only by complete with Jesus as the living identification with Jesu as the living Bread that sharing in the life becomes possible" (Dunn, *Eerdman's Commentary*, 1178).

34. "A length of time roughly equal to the potential of a person or the equivalent of the complete renewal of a human population. The definition itself was initially employed by the Etruscans and was construed as a period of time from the moment that happened until the point in time that all people who once lived at the first moment had died. At that point a new speculum commences" (*Oxford English Dictionary*).

word soon was displaced by the Vulgate transliteration of *aeternum* which has no current English equivalent.

Galatians 1:5

ὦ ἡ δόξα εις τους αίωνας των αίωνων ἀμην

Cui gloria in specula saeculorum. Amen. (*Nestle-Aland Novum Testament Latine*)

"Whom be glory for the eons of the eons. Amen!" (CLNT)

The Pauline prologue doxology engages our mind with this august eulogy. Was this placed in the text for emphasis, or was this the usual salutation? By way of observation and inspection the "doxa" is the same word as "gloria" in the Latin, which is the normative singular feminine noun; basically the glory is naming the subject, in this case God and Father of our Lord Jesus Christ. In the absolute sense it means "to them be the highly favorable opinion throughout the eons," with the superlative supplied for emphasis. Over 19 occurrences this word is used 12 times alone in the Book of Revelation.[35] Furthermore we engage the text in relation to its contextual usage.

Revelation 4:9

Καΐ όταν δώσουν τά ζωα δοξαν και τιμήν καεύχαριστιαν τω καυηυενω επι του υρονω τω ζωντι εις τους αιώνας των αιώνων

Et cum darent ill animalia gloriam et honarem et gratiarum actioned sedenti super thorium, viventi in secular saculorum.

"And Whenever the living creatures give glory and honor and thanks to him who is seated on the throne who lives for ever and ever." (ESV)

This text clearly exhibits the idea that the Lamb that sat on the throne is ascribed the superlative for the eons into the eons. Here the text speaks of an angelic host singing the creation anthem, ascribing to the Lamb that was slain a reign for the eons of the eons. This advocates for the term for ever and ever, as it appears that in the absolute sense he will reign forever. But why the superlative, because the first "ever" is limited to the second?

---

35. Gal 1:4, 5, Phil 4:20; 1 Tim 1:17, 2 Tim 4:18, Heb 13:21, 1 Pet 4:11, 5:11; Rev 1:6, 4:9, 4:10, 5:13, 14, 7:12, 10:6, 11:15, 15:7, 19:3, 20:10, 22:5. See *Young's Analytical Concordance* (Cambridge, UK: Lutterworth, 1967), 311.

ἄιδις, αἰών IN THE GREEK SCRIPTURES

The first one takes into consideration the past, and the second takes into consideration the millennium and beyond.

The problem with the transliteration of the word *aeternum* is that when it is transliterated into English for "eternal, for ever and ever," it becomes problematic, as with *olam* and *aeon* which have a distinct beginning, middle part, and end. As Cox rightly affirms, "Aeons and Atonal denotes periods, ages, of time, however vast, which sooner or later come to a close."[36] This is exactly what we are arguing, that this is a duration which is in fact limited, and should be treated as such. Yet Christ must reign until he places all enemies under his feet.[37]

Furthermore, *aeon* could not be passed as a synonym for eternal. Thus, we contend that even in this particular context in which the word is used, there is no sustainable evidence that the word here referred to eternity. So let's revisit this text in another way. The usage of eons of the eons is not placed in the text for emphatic purpose, but it takes into consideration all the eons before in its plural form and looks to future eons. The grammatical agreements attest to this: the first *aiōnas* is an accusative plural masculine noun. The accusative identifies or makes an accusation of what the subject did. In the temple scene, it is the Lamb that sits on the throne and is going to reign. The *aiōnōn* is also a noun, but genitive plural masculine. This indicates that the genitive is a description of the preceding noun (declensions). The noun is "reign" and that reign is for only a period of time. It could not speak of "forever," for the last monarch, the one to suffer the dethronement of death, is not the subject of Revelation 4. Thus the living creatures in the text are genuflecting to the one sitting on the throne, and they employed the superlative for the eons (plural), taking into consideration the past to the future eons (plural). On this powerful temple scene, Knoch's comments highlight that this captures the thought in this verb, and asserts that the original Syriac version provides an accurate rendering to this particular text.[38]

---

36. Cox, *Salvator Mundi*, 102.

37. 1 Cor 15:20–28.

38. "The Elder and the animals are *brought*, not redeemed. The celebrate Israel's deliverance. The failure to note this distinction and consequent attempt to reconcile the two parts of this song, has led to much confusion in the manuscripts. It has been suggested that the Syriac Version preserves the true rendering here. After "blessing|" it goes right on and gives every creature to the Lambkin, rather than getting praise from them, thus (combined with Vaticanus 'b' And honer and glory and blessing And every creature which heaven And on the earth and underneath the earth And on the sea and all [those]

Doctrine of the Eons

We will press further with our inquiry in relation to this specific word and its plural and noun form as it is highlighted in the New Testament. As Ramelli and Konstan further argued, the word αἰωνας did not reflect endlessness in its duration, except when it spoke of God, and it did not prove in any way that it reflected the age of God.[39] Could it be possible that the ancients were mistaken where this word is concerned, and that "eternity" is a perfectly acceptable word in the English language and Bibles? Notwithstanding the veracity of the argument, the fact stands for itself that this word in itself clearly did not express "endless" in its original form. Nor did the classics and some of the early patristics express this in such a way.[40] Samuel Cox shared this view as he noted the inconsistency of the common translations in their view of this word αἰωνας.[41] We argue this case, but it clearly demonstrates the absurdity of scholastic infidelity. The αἰωνας in its entries did not convey the word "eternal" in any sense. Furthermore the word "eternal" could not be used in soteriology, nor concerning the life of man (anthropology), nor of future (eschatological) punishment, as supposed by some New Testament linguistics. Stevenson highlighted this point further, saying that the usage of these words used in judgment texts did not express eternity.[42]

---

in them! and I hear all [Messengers] saying "To. him who sitting in the throne-To the Lambkin—Be blessing and honor and glory and might for eons of the eons" (Knoch, *Concordant Commentary*, 388–89).

39. "αἰωνας carries the meaning 'everlasting' in deriving from accompanying adjectives" (Ramelli and Konstan, *Terms For Eternity*, 59).

40. "αἰών In the New Testament is listed to denote the ages which denote the past, present and the future of this word, so the adjective should follow that usage except modifying God. Consequently, these words which do not mean 'endless' cannot prove the endlessness of God, for then they would also prove the endlessness of sinners. His eternity however is proved by his character which is revealed in the name YHWH" (Ramelli and Konstan, *Terms For Eternity*, 59).

41. "αἰώνας therefore means, and must mean belonging to an epoch, or the epoch ; and αἰώνας χόλασις You have now, besides your common sense, high authors for believing that they do not imply endlessness whether in Scripture or out of it; they always carry in them the suggestion of periods and epochs of time" (Cox, *Salvator Mundi*, 122).

42. "The doxologies employ the term as 'blessed,' 'honor,' 'glory,' and 'praise,' calling for worship of the deity and contain no contextual evidence respecting the time element If these read be read as ascriptions of praise and call worship God thought the coming ages viewed as the best periods of humanity's history, There is no difficulties Aries either linguistically or theologically. There is no suggestion that worship will cease at the end of the ages mentioned in the New Testament, but speculation beyond that point ventures outside the biblical frame. Of the nine examples of he polytotonic phrase in Revelation four refer to the Deity living 'unto the ages off the ages', two too 'smoke sending form

ἀίδις, αἰών IN THE GREEK SCRIPTURES

The preceding arguments sought to postulate the argument that the expression αἰώνας did not express endlessness, whether in the past, present, or future. Furthermore, we sought to prove this in a number of ways, such as the mode we engage in how this word is used in a number of New Testament texts, although we did not exhaustively engage all the New Testament texts to which this word is employed. Suffice to say, we in turn provided sufficient evidence that this word did not express "eternity" when reading these texts contextually. We did not provide a full treatment of the amount of biblical text, as this is not what we set out to do. Rather we engaged with a number of selective texts to provide the basis of our assumption, and we did not rely on my own interpretation, but rather we visited a number of scholars through which we exegetically engaged. We also consulted a number of scholastic works. We are aware of our own parochialism in order to get a prevaricated answer to how aeon and aeons were employed. We discovered that there is a large preponderance within Western thinkers and scholars alike, who suggested that this word meant other than what the word meant in the original Greek. Nevertheless, we consulted contemporaries of the nineteenth-century biblical exegetes of the likes of Samuel Cox and John Wesley Hanson. Their soundness of ratiocination brought breath and bravado, as well as some depth in understanding further how this word was used among the classics and in the New Testament. Consequently, the basis of the contention provided by Ramelli and Konstan further buttress the argument that this lone word αἰών, αἰώνας in its original context did not express eternity nor did the classics express it that way. We noted that the word used in its absolute sense meant eternity, in spite of the polyvalence usage in our English Bibles, yet in this sense it referred to God and only in that sense could the meaning "eternal and forever" from the Greek word be used. We at this juncture will be looking into how the word "eternal" is employed in Western thought before we encounter the "hell" text, which others have used as a proof text for conscious torment and annihilation. We want to hear the polemic arguments that suggest otherwise. The next chapter will look past the word eternal and ask whether this is true to the original.

---

punishing of eh devotees of the wild beast' and from the destruction and the torment of Satan, the reign of Christ and of his people with (Rev 4:9 and 10 10:6; 15:7; 14:11; 19:3; 20:, 11, 15 22:5). In respect to Reve 4:, 10:106), and the fourth (Rev 15:2–7) in section of four sentences contains more than a dozen O.T expressions, the influence of the Hebrew through and language must be recognized and once OT contains no reference to 'eternity' it appears improbable that the seer of the Apocalypse was thinking in terms of infinite duration" (Stevenson, *Time and Eternity,* 60–61).

II

Eternal

THIS CHAPTER WILL LOOK at Western thought and how the Hebrew and Greek exegete and scholastic works employ this word; could they refute that *olam* and *aion* did not denote or even express endlessness? We will demonstrate that the word did not express endlessness and "forever" meant "forever." Much of this we already discussed, but for the sake of thoroughness we want to engage wider works to see whether this word meant eternal. *Eth* (עת) is the most common Hebrew word typically translated "time." Again *eth* does not refer to "time" as a dimension or even as a long period of time; rather it refers to a definite moment or short period of time. This is indicated by its common use with prepositions such as *in, at, for, to, from, up to* and the adjective is coupled with a demonstrative pronoun to refer to a particular comment in the past or sometimes in the future ("at that time"). *Eth* often refers to the time to do something.[1] Furthermore, the emphasis on the content rather than abstract notions of time is also indicated by the employment of generation (*dor, gena*), which refers both to a person's life span (considered roughly 40 or 33 years) and to a group of people who lived at the same time. Many of the commandments in the Pentateuch are enjoined upon people "through your generations" (Exod 12:14). Expressions such as "generations" are synonymous with "forever." Even with the words for *olam*, variously translated in the NRSV as "forever,

---

1. Gen 24:11; Hos 10: 12 Eccl 3:108 or sometimes happens (Lev 15:25; Ruth 2:14; 1 Sam 4:20 It I sometimes coupled with a modifier to describe the moment or period such as "the time of your distress" Judges 10:14, "time of suffering" New. 9:27 "evil time" (Psalm 37:19; Amos 5:13) Sakenfield edit el vol.5, 596–597.

"eternal," "everlasting," and "perpetual," one must be careful not to impose a strict abstract philosophical concept, for example, an "eternity" that encompasses or transcends time. Rather, *olam* typically refers to a "long or remote time in the future."[2] The basic sense of the Greek word *aiōn* (αιών) is the relative time associated with something such as a person's life or a generation in the sense of an "age," *gena* ("generation"). Hence the word *aiōn* and the adjective *aiōnios* (αιώνας) resemble use of *olam* in the Old Testament. Similarly, they may also have the sense of "in perpetuity" and thus be translated "forever" or "eternal" (John 8:35); this is especially the case with the doxological affirmations that mirror the sentiments of the Psalms.[3] Charles Baker refutes the idea that the word "eternal" is limited in its duration; he used Moulton and Milligan's *Vocabulary of the Greek New Testament*.[4] Baker contends that "in spite of the meaning being limited to a life span, in his view, the fact remains that the word meant "eternal."[5] Furthermore, Baker argues in his view "God's creatures exist in time and as long as they exist time exist."[6] This is akin to nonsense, because it makes

---

2. "*Olam* is used with the preposition "until" and"to" "for" when it refers to the future. That future may be short as a person's lifetime: "He shall be brought to the door or the doorpost, and his master shall pierce his ear with an awl; and he shall serve him for life(Exod 21:6) While it is often translated by the English "forever" and its synonyms, it is used often in hyperbolic. This is exemplified by the psalmist and other poetic writers, who asserts that "we will bless the Lord this time evermore" (Ps 115:18; 125:2, 131:3 Isa 59:21)" (Sakenfield, *Interpreters Dictionary of the Bible*, 598).

3. Gal 1:5; Phil 4:20; Jude 25. "Aion as the time of the world elides with a nation of the "world" itself (1Cor 1:20), Paul parallels aiōn (age) is also translated "world" (e.g., Mark 4:19; Rom 12:2; 2Cor 4:4)" (Sakenfield, *Interpreters Dictionary of the Bible*, 599).

4. "αιώνας the etymological note on αιών in Grimm-Tayler, though less antiquated than usual suggest an addition of a statement often the side (Latin aevum) three collateral declensions from the same routine the Sanskit dyu and its Zen equivalent the idea if life, especially life. Predominates. So its the Germanic donates (aiw) The Word, whose roots it is of course fruit to dig, when it may of meant "Long Life" or "old age" perhaps the last attracts idea we can define fruit in the prehistoric c period, so as to account for its derives. In general the word depicts that which the horizon is not in view, whether the horizon be at an infinite distance, or whether it lies no faster than the span of a Caesar's life" (Moulton and Milligan, *Vocabulary of the Greek*, 16).

5. "It is important to have a proper concept of time and eternity, space, matter, and time Arte all involved in creation. It would seem impossible to have any one without the others. Before God created there was noo space, matter or time. As long as creator endures all three of these things will endure, there can be no end time without blotting out and redoing to nothingness of everything that God created" (Baker, *Dispensational Theology*, 643).

6. "Methods of measuring time will ever come when there will been succession of events. With this fact in mind, the only way man can express eternity is to speak of

no sense! To which end, Baker's exegetical task of understanding this word becomes problematic as he does not give reason for time to exist or man to exist, and this in itself is an exegetical conundrum. Robert Peterson, an evangelical theologian and proponent of hell, noted that the word *olam* did not express endlessness; he sought to prove that the word "eternal" was mentioned in a number of places in the Hebrew Bible.[7] Consequently by admission, the context determines the meaning of a specific word and in this case eternity should not be used as endless in specific texts. Peterson justified his argument by quoting Psalm 90:2, in which—and we agree when speaking of God in the absolute sense as aforesaid—"eternal" can be safely attested.

Furthermore, when taking into consideration this word eternal it poses a number of difficulties in the vernacular of our language. Western scholars agree that the word "eternal" in relation to the Deity is in the absolute sense and in selected passages of biblical text. Yet in unrelated texts, the rendering becomes obscure. Girdlestone openly confesses that this word need to be met with caution.[8] Girdlestone noted the occurrences of the Hebrew and Greek word should be met with care, especially the usage of the word when referring to Deity, but he also demonstrated that it was rather difficult to interpret all of these Old Testament texts when it comes to humanity and soteriology. I agree, with Girdlestone's view, as he clearly understood that this word did not express eternity, and that it would be foolhardy to translate this word without taking into consideration the context.

---

time rolling on in endless succession and this is exactly what the Scripture does when it uses expression as the eons of the eons. Needless to say, the stent in Revelation 10:6, "that there should be time no longer" does not meant that time itself was to cease, but that there should be no further delay" (Baker, *Dispensational Theology*, 643).

7. "Everlasting" Does not always mean "everlasting" This is the only occurrence of the words "everlasting life" in the Old Testament, although the concept of God's people enjoying life in the presence after death is taught such as Job 19:26, Psalm 73:23, 24, and Isaiah 26:19. Here in Daniel 12:2 the word "everlasting" (Hebrew *Olam*) is used to *describe the fate of the just and the unjust. This word serves carful study, as it does not always means "everlasting". It was an adjective signifying long duration with limits set by the context."* Peterson, *Hell on Trial,* 34–35.

8. "We understand very little about the future about the relation of human life to the rest of existence and abut the moral weight of unbelief, as viewed in the light of eternity. If on the one hand, it is wrong to add to God's word, on the other hand we must not take away from it; and if we stagger under the doctrine of eternal punishment as it set forth in Scripture, we must be content with, cleaving to the Gospel of God's love in Christ, while acknowledging that there is a dark background which we are unable to comprehend" (Girdlestone, *Synonyms of the Old Testament*, 319).

I think many evangelical scholars have chosen to do this when taking into consideration this word; there appears to be a bias which leads to ignoring the word. However, Edward William Fudge argues, "we should probably conclude that both the word "eternal" and *aiōnios* have root signifying time, in both English (and its Latin ancestor) and in the Greek. But some are ready to than to remind us that the biblical interpretation the important thing is not secular etymology as much as hared usage."[9] According to Fudge, the Greek word *aiōnios* is "forever" yet he perceives that its usage should be "within the limits of the possibility inherent in the person or thing itself."[10] Fudge further points out the notion in his view that the Bible employs the word *aiōnios* to be construed with the Trinity, as well as redemption. What he means is that this word is to be understood in light of the Trinity as to soteriology and anthropology and eschatology.[11] This is true, as Fudge attests.[12]

Fudge's own assessment of this word demonstrates that the word could not be perceived as "eternal," but as a quality of life; this is what the New Testament sought to express when speaking of the life of humanity, it sought to express the quality of life as opposed to punishment and endless life. Why, Fudge argues, do all New Testament scholars tend to agree with this word, but when it comes to endless punishment they seem to agree in its application to hell?[13] Clearly we sought to engage with this matter

---

9. "Nicole observes that 51 times in the New Testament, *aiōnios* applies to "eternal felicity" of the redeemed sand there art is conceded by all the limitation of time applies. On the other hand Pétavel insist that at least 70 times in the Bible Fudge p39so that it signifies only "and indeterminate duration of which the maximum is fixed by the intrinsic nature of the persons or things" (Fudge, *Fire That Consumes*, 39).

10. Fudge, *Fire That Consumes*, 39–40.

11. "It is obvious that this word is used in a qualitative sense. this seems to reflect one common Jewish attitude about history and the last things" Fudge, *Fire That Consumes*, 40).

12. "Eternal Punishment or "Eternal" fire are and punishment which "partake of the nature of the *aiōn* what are peculiar to the realm and the nature of God. "The real point is the "character of the punishment." It is "that order of the Age to come as contrasted with any earthly penalties. "When the New Testament speaks of "eternal" Life, in this view, the adjective aiōnios refers to the quality more than to the length of life" (Fudge, *Fire That Consumes*, 42).

13. "Eternal" describes both Guilty and quantity, character and duration, what precisely does it describe in the case if final punishment? Traditionalist and conditionalist may shake hands in agreement concerning the word, but they immediately draw swords when they begin to apply it to hell. The wicked go into eternal punishment. Does that refer to eh act of retribution or to its effect? Which is-eternal the punishing or the

Doctrine of the Eons

with reputable scholars; we have deduced that the word "eternal" itself was problematic. However, Fudge, in his work *The Fire that Consumes*, sought to provide the perfect rationale for this word "eternal" but came up with a white elephant in the room by employing existential biblical scholars to buttress his argument. It appears that their refining of this word is only to justify the argument that the only justifiable way that this word could be used is when we talked about "hell." Outside of that the word could only be used as "a quality state of being, and not life in itself."[14] Talbot, however, notes that this word meant eternal in the absolute sense when speaking of God, yet when speaking of "eternal punishment" he is of the view of Barclay in his "New Testament Words": "it is remedial and in no way suggests endlessness."[15]

In summation, we engaged with a number of scholars in relation to the word "eternal." The problem that we encountered is that the word appeared in relation to God in the absolute sense. However, in relation to the doctrine of soteriology and hematology, it was met with a questionable trajectory. As Fudge rightly argues, it appeared to define the word "eternal" as a state of being or quality of life. I think he means the "life to the full." Furthermore, Fudge's treatment of the text that he presents has a number of issues, though so far, from the vantage point of his own scholastic proclivity, it appears that his exegetical judgment was prohibited by his own evangelical parochialism. His testament of the nuance of the word "eternal" was limited, and this may be due to the source that he chose to explain this word. He is not clear when speaking of *aiōnis* with "the Trinity," as he linked it with salvation, redemption, and anthropology, and we are not sure

---

punishment" (Fudge, *Fire That Consumes*, 43–44).

14. "Of the 70 usages of the adjective "eternal" (*aiōnios*) in the New Testament, six times the word qualifies nouns signifying acts or processes, as distinct from persons or things. These cases call for special consideration. The are "|eternal Judgment (Heb 5:9), "Eternal redemption" (Heb 9:12) "Eternal judgment" (Heb 6:2) "Eternal sin"(Mark 3:29), "Eternal punishment" (Matthew 25:46)and "eternal destruction" (2Thess 1:9) Three occur in Hebrews; all six have to do with final judgment and its outcome. Here we see again the *other-age* quality of the "eternal". There is something transcendent, eschatological, divine about this judgment, this sin this punishment and destruction, redemption and salvation will have no end. `if in one sense these things are *timeless, they are another sense without temporal* limits,. They belong to that age to Come which is not bound by time and which will never end. Fudge, *Fire That Consumes*, 44.

15. "Eternal punishment is simply punishment of any duration that has its causal source in the eternal purpose of God. As Barclay himself puts it, "Eternal punishment is—literally that kind for Remedial punishment which befits God to give which only God can give"" (Talbott, *Inescapable Love of God* (1999), 83, Barclay, *Daily Study Bible*, 35).

if this was merely a pun. Fudge clearly demonstrated that *aiōnios* succinctly carries a qualitative sense. He suggests in his view that it is "something that partakes of the transcendent realm of divine activity. It indicates a relationship between kingdom of God and the Age to Come, to the eschatological realties which in Jesus had begun already manifest themselves in the present age."[16] This brings us to the "hell" teaching of Scriptures. We will seek to bring balanced scholastic views and polemic arguments in this vein.

---

16. Fudge, *Fire That Consumes*, 66.

12

Hell
The Theology of Hell

THE PRESENT TEACHING OF what happens when you die has been met with strong convictions from both sides, theological conservatives and liberals alike. Those who oppose the theology of hell have been met with suspicion and treated as unorthodox or heretical. I will look at Bradley Jersak's thesis, *Her Gates Will Never Shut.'* Jersak conducts a thorough investigation into the word "hell." However, whether we agree or disagree with Jersak, he challenges the status quo of Western orthodoxy (so-called), unlike Walls' work on *Heaven, Hell and Purgatory*. This work is Catholic in tone, which limits the scope of his research to present the facts as they are rather than post a hypothetical epistemology which is hampered because of scholastic bias.

Consequently then, my approach was to understand the root meaning of this word, and then engage with selective texts in which often the meaning seems somewhat obscure to the average reader of the Scriptures. Therefore, it is incumbent upon a thorough investigative inquiry into this word "hell," and from it we can deduce a conclusive argument. Let us look at the etymological root word before we engage in any of the scholastic trajectories that are out there. According to BDAG,[1] Sheol is the underworld, or a place of inquiry. According to BARG,[2] *adhz* the proper noun, is the

---

1. Brown, *Hebrew and English Lexicon*, 982.
2. Bauers, *Greek-English Lexicon of the New Testament*, 16.

name of the god of the underworld as the place of the dead. In *Synonyms of the Old Testament*, Robert Girdlestone opined, "the state which we call death, in other words the condition consequent upon the act of dying, is viewed in three aspects Kever, meaning corruption of the physical body, Shachath when the body dissolved, Sheol is the locality of the departed and Hades, however he argued that the meaning was uncertain."[3] Peterson argued that "it may have derived from other ancient cultures."[4] The words Sheol and Hades have a different root word and the word "hell" comes from another definition that differs from the Hebrew and Greek. Peterson does not agree with such a premise, as in his view he tabulated that "'Sheol had two meanings: originally it meant "grave" and its later came to mean "hell" the righteous share the former, the wicked, but only the wicked populate the latter."[5] Jersak employs another Hebrew term called the "deep, (*Tehom*), this Sematic terms is often referred to the "Submerge Chaos ("sea"), the primordial deep described in Genesis 1:2."[6] However, we will notice that it comes to us from the Anglo-Saxons who became Christians in medieval times. The word *Hel* was translated from the Latin word *infernus*, "the lower region" and designated the fiery place for the damned. Yet how did Hel designate before the conversion of the Anglo-Saxons? The root behind this word came from a tribe of Scandinavians and Icelanders, converted from paganism to Christianity long after the Anglo-Saxons, who are called Norse and who used this word *Hel*. The Old Norse Hell is a place of oath-breakers, other evil persons, and those who were unlucky enough to have died in old age rather than in the glory of the battlefield. Thus, the Indo-European root behind the Old English Hel and Old Norse Hel—with its Germanic

---

3. Girdlestone R.B. *Synonyms of the Old Testament*, 28.

4. I noted that Robert `Peterson highlighted a key point "There a variety of translations that point toward an ever greater variety of approaches to Sheol. One approach assumes that the Israelites shard the mythological ideas concerning the afterlife of Mesopotamia and Egypt`:` `the Israelites speculations, though restrained in comparison rot the ancient peoples. Evangelicals reject this approach because it leave God and his sepia revelation rot Israel out of the picture. Peterson, 27.

5. Peterson, 2.

6. Jersak argues that their is a metaphorical connection with this terminology sued in the Septuagint, where the mythical "leviathan" and the /greek "*abussous*" Early Judaism and the Greek Scriptures shift the meaning of *Them* and "*abussos*" *into a prison for disobedient spirits,* Furthermore Jersak contends, that in the N?T the Abyss together with two Hebrew Scriptures derivative, creates the imagery of chaotic sea/fiery-pit. On the one hand, the Abyss is equal to the Old Testament *Them* as a source of a rival chaos. In Revelation, the Beast actually come up out of the Abyss (9:1, 2)11:7, 17:18), parallel to the emergence of the dragon and the beast from lout of sea (*thalasses*-12:18; 13:1). Jersak, 24.

relatives like German *hodielle* "to conceal or cover"—contains hole, hollow, helmet, and to cover, conceal from the classical Latin verb for "to hide." Fudge used Gagster's work to note discrepancies in the Hebrew.[7] Fudge agreed with Gagster's definition and that the word had different meanings, but the root is the same as aforestated, "to ask or inquire."

However, Knoch argues, "Hell is transient, when the Great White Throne (Rev 20:13, 14), so too, with hades. It gives up its dead and is confined to the Lake of fire which is the second death. Hence it is the reason for spirit substitution of death for Hades."[8] Consequently, Fudge agreed with the aforementioned statements concerning the Germanic roots of the word hell. He suggests "the German Holle comes from Hohle, a cavern (kin to "hole" in English). The Greek hadēs literally means the "unseen" realm. The English word "hell" comes from the Anglo-Saxon Helen, which meant "to cover" or "to hide."[9]

Balthasar, in *Dare We Hope that All Men Be Saved?*, argues that Aquinas's view of hell was eternity but by the time of[10] Augustine's view on hell in *De Genesi ad Litteram Libri XII*—an influence it is said that may have come from Porphyry—it can be said broadly speaking that hell is primarily one of imagination.[11] It could be understood that hell is a state and not a place.

How then did the evangelical church in the West miss this, and still hold onto the evangelical definition of Hell, which can be defined thus: In the old conception, Sheol is the place of the dead for all people, both righteous and unrighteous. It is the point of inquiry, or "asks."[12] In Jesus's teaching, however, we find mention of a place of postmortem punishment in contrast with a place of reward (often "heaven"). In the New Testament,

---

7. "The word "Sheol" does not appear in any non-Hebrew Semitic literature yet discovered, other than as a loan-word from Hebrew. The etymology is uncertain. Most modern scholars seem to think it comes from root meaning "ask" or "inquire"." Fudge, *Fires That Consume*, 82.

8. Knoch, *Problem of Evil*, 42–43.

9. Fudge, *Fires That Consume*, 83.

10. Balthasar's reliance on Aquinas's explanation is largely conditioned by his times; he keeps to the notion of "endlessness" in the sense it assumes changes in the forms of punishment. See Balthasar, *Dare We Hope*, 98.

11. Balthasar went further: he contends that there is difficulty a real hell, but I take it to affect the imagination, not the body. See Balthasar, *Dare We Hope*, 99.

12. This suggests that the Hebrews would query where do the dead go, at the time of death? The answers were obscured in the Hebrew Scriptures, hence the thought of "ask" or "inquiry" was tabulated.

there is some distinction between gehenna and Hades; later Christian reflection fleshed out these ideas and generally combined the ideas of gehenna and Hades into that of Hell.[13] Mounce does not offer any reason for how the Greek word evolved into how we have it today. Vine defines Hades as "the region of departed spirits of the lost" (but including the blessed dead in periods preceding the ascension of Christ, it has been thought by some that the words etymologically meant "the unseen" (from a negative and *eidô*, "to see"), but this cavalier derivation is questionable; a more provable derivation is from *hadô*, signifying "all-receiving." It corresponds to "Sheol" in the Old Testament; in the KJV Old Testament and New Testament it has been unhappily rendered "hell."[14] According to *The Baker Illustrated Bible Dictionary* hell is defined as: "The place where the lost are assigned by God to eternal punishment of both body and soul (Matt 10:28)." "This agony of eternal torment in hell is the greatest of all possible tragedies. At times there is confusion about this topic, since the English word "hell" is used different ways in our English Bible. Sometimes, it is used to translate the Hebrew word Sheol or the Greek word hades, which refers generally to the place of the departed dead. Other times it used more properly to translate the Aramaic derived the Greek *hades*, which refers generally to the place of the departed dead. Other times they infer the Aramaic derived the Greek Gehenna which refers to the place of eternal punishment of the wicked following the final punishment . . ."[15] In light of this inclusive contention in relation to Gehenna, Jarsak's argument noted that it is Gehenna that had shaped the theological trajectory of Western thought more than the message of Jesus.[16] Jersak further elucidated his argument by providing the historical content and location of Gehenna: "by the time the gorge became a byword, a layered backstory had developed many generations of firm conflict."[17] Jersak hitherto posits the idea that Gehenna provides

---

13. Mounce, *Complete Expository Dictionary*, 219.

14. Vines, *New Testament Greek Grammar*, 382.

15. Longman, *Baker Illustrated Bible Dictionary*, 765.

16. Jersak contends, "Our understanding-or lack thereof—of Gehenna traditions(s) shapes our view of hell and judgment. More than that, it profoundly influences our understanding of Jesus' message and ministry" (*Her Gates Will Never Be Shut*, 35).

17. "Gehenna is a gorge that bends around the West and south sides of the Old or First Walls of Jerusalem like an L, right beneath the hill we know as Mount Zion. From Jerusalem 's Zion and Dung Gates, one could peer down into the valley known in OT times ads "Valley of the Sons of Hinnom" (Josh 15:8). the valley depends from the West slide of Jerusalem (Wadi-el-Mes), then bends eastwards across the Southside (Wadi-Er

a metaphor for spiritual destruction: "Jesus also appears to add a realize eschatological and personal dimension, as a metaphor for spiritual looseness and the torment of alienation from God. For Jersak, in his view takes It to be the barometer for today and for the future, from which one can be saved."[18] These thoughts are considered by prominent Western evangelicals as future punishment, or "the eternal hell fire." Fudge noted that "the mythological Hades was a god of the underworld, then the name of the nether world itself."[19]

At this juncture, from the aforementioned statements we have highlighted that we have encountered a number of issues that have been raised from the definition; one point that is evident is that the translations of the Hebrew and the Greek word simply ignored the root word, i.e., where this word actually came from. We noted that the word entries offered up by evangelical scholars are rather deceptive as they only give us half of the truth; therefore, we have to conduct deconstruction and demythologization by peeling off the layers of evangelical myths in order to arrive at a coherent understanding. Furthermore, we need to look at where it started from, note if the words were unfluenced by Anglo-Saxon or Norse usage which was simply ignored; for example, the biblical word for the realm of the dead is not consciousness as that is the realm of the living—when you are dead you are dead. Period. Baer noted hell is a late entry into the English Bible, but finds its rooted in Greek mythology.[20] Furthermore, Baer argued, "The tradition of fiery Hell has deep roots in Greek mythology and

---

Rabbi), where it meets the Kidron ravine near the lower pool of Siloam at the southeastern corner of the city" (Jersak, *Her Gates Will Never Be Shut*, 34). I felt that Jersak provided some invaluable research in his thesis, and that it was well worth noting. Read the entire chapter 3 for further commentary on this subject.

18. Jersak, *Her Gates Will Never Be Shut*, 61.

19. Hadēs comes into biblical usage when Septuagint translators chose it to represent the Hebrew Sheol., an Old Testament Sheol, too received all the dead, the Old Testament has no specific division there involving either punishment or reward. Intertestamental Judaism held at least two options on Hades. Those who expected a partial resurrection(of the righteous only) Saw Hades as everlasting (for the wicked); those who looked for a general resurrection naturally through off it as temporary" (Fudge, *Fire That Consumes*, 205).

20. "The doctrine of Hell, as we know it today, didn't begin too really grew till the 5th century, possibly even later. The modern English word for Hell didn't actually come to exist until the year 725 CE" (Baer, *What the Hell*, 44).

many different religions. It was popularized to become what we supposed of today's Dante Divine Comedy written in the early fourteenth century."[21]

The Jews in the Hebrew Scriptures have no notion of life beyond the grave; such ideas were a matter of inquiry, that is, "where do the dead go when they die?" And as such there was no knowledge of what was beyond the grave, hence the Psalms state there is no knowledge of them that go down into Sheol. Later on, between the Second Temple and the 400-year gap when the Jews became Hellenistic, they developed gnostic ideas and concepts into their psyche as well as immortality as a word; this was not a Jewish but a Greek concept which was adopted by the Jews in the late first century BCE.

By the time of Jesus's entry on the earth, the Jews had developed all sorts of mythical ideas and notions about the realm of the dead. William Crockett, contributor for *Four Views on Hell*, also argued in the same view; he suggested that "fire is often nonliteral in Jewish writings; they employed colorful language to make a point. Even the Torah to have been written with "black fire on white fire" (Jerusalem Justin Martyr Talmud Shekalim 6:1, 49d) . . . " He further argues that "Jewish and early Christian writings is regularly used to create a mood of seriousness or reverence, often have little to do with the material world of intense heat."[22] Much of these ideas took on new shape and form in the time of Jesus and among the religious leaders of the first century. Crockett opined that "when Jewish thought wedded to Hellenistic culture, we often find Jewish writers interpreting metaphorically, as in Aristobulus, a second-century BC Jewish document."[23] This is clearly exhibited in the parables told by Jesus, i.e., the rich man and the beggar at the gate in Luke 16:19–31. How then does this thought develop into the Christian thinking? Justin Martyr, the patriarch of Menus (100–165 AD) and one of the greatest apologetics of the Christian faith, postulated that the wicked will be damned into a conscious torment; it is his own words that shaped and formed the thinking of Western theology even today. Within the early patristic period, regarding Christ's *descensus* (descent into Hades), Jersak highlighted the point that Hades in the thought of the early church was a place that held the souls captive; therefore, it needed to be destroyed

---

21. "Dante writes about his travels through Hell, Purgatory, and Heaven. Hell is called inferno" (Baer, *What the Hell*, 44–45).

22. Gundry et al., *Four Views on Hell*, 53.

23. Gundry et al., *Four Views on Hell*, 53.

Doctrine of the Eons

and robbed of its good—I take this to mean that he was speaking of all the souls that had died and gone to Hades.[24]

Throughout the decades, the doctrine for hell has never being consistent or clear; this view is argued by Crockett in the book *Four Views on Hell*. He postulated the metaphorical view, by suggesting that "the images of Hell that we discover in the New Testament, was given for the purpose of enabling the reader not to view these as literal picture of torment, but symbolic one. He further contended that in both Jewish and Greek literature, contrived and propounded vivid pictures of hell, but notably they did not intend their descriptions to be taken literally."[25] Arguably this argument is not shared by all: Paul Enns argued on the thought of Hades that "in the intertestamental period there developed a two compartment theory, (probably an influence from Persian Zoroastrianism), which taught that Sheol and Hades had two compartment, a place of bliss for the righteous and a place of torment for the wicked. The righteous were waiting for the resurrection of Christ, who then delivered them form Hades into God's presence."[26] According to Walls, "The Doctrine of Eternal Hell is "eternal," is an entirely contingent truth, which is to say, because according to his view the scriptures teaches it . . . eternal hell is due not in any way to the lack of grace opportunity but rather to the *rejection* of grace opportunity."[27]

On the basis of the above statements, Enns further contends that the exact meaning of this word "Hades" is inconclusive, as it serves a dichotomic function in the New Testament. Christopher W. Morgan stated in a word of caution that "Hell as punishment vividly depicts God as judge who justly sentences the wicked. Hell as the place of destruction. He further argues portrays God as the warrior or victor who defeats his enemies. Hell as banishment views God as the King who allows only his citizens in his kingdom."[28] From Morgan's premise, we understand that his herme-

---

24. Jersak argued "on Holy Saturday (Eph 4:8–9, 1 Pet 3:18–2; 4:6) was healed widely, even entering our creed. There was a plethora of interpretations as to what this actually meant (for example, Cyril, John of Damascene, Gregory of Nyssa, Augustine, and Aquinas), yet the poplar hope was that Jesus invaded Hades n out suffer further but to conquer its gates and rescue the dead" (Jersak, *Her Gates Will Never Be Shut*, 19).

25. Crockett, *Four Views on Hell*, 78–81.

26. Enns, *Moody Handbook of Theology*, 393.

27. "To in insist that eternal hell is true, even of it requires that some persons receive little relatively little opportunity to be save is to place the doctrine on a very dubious foundation" (Walls, *Heaven, Hell and Purgatory*, 209).

28. Morgan, *Is Hell for Real*, 46.

neutic lens is tinted with the views of evangelical theological epistemology, thereby rendering it ineffective to give a definitive term on hell as he views it in light of the atonement and Trinity.

What we find currently is that that those who hold to the view on hell simply ignore Scripture by proof-texting their own scholastic trajectories within the parameters of holy writ. Is there a conclusive argument to this, we may ask? What we have understood by the root definition is that "hell" is the place of inquiry; in the Greek it is the abode or realm of the departed spirits; in Middle English it was used as a place of cover, therefore quite naturally that which was covered becomes unseen! "The Unseen" fit perfectly the idea between these two definitions; later definitions of hell were added by the traditions of the world.

Consequently then, are we arguing about doing away with the popular view of hell? Not really, but it would help if you reconsider the implications of the theology of Hell, and ask, what would your being look like at the end of your life? The question may strike a chord, as we are all aware we do not know what is on the other side of this vast chasm between heaven/ earth and beneath. Peterson concedes that popular text that has a traditional evangelical reading must be read in light of its appropriate context and nuances.[29]

Evangelical theology holds to two views on Hell. The most widely held view within Christian history was expostulated notably by Tertullian,[30] Augustine, Anselm, and Jonathan Edwards: hell is eternal conscious punishment. Many understand this punishment as mental and spiritual. The main argument is, in the New Testament fire (Matt 25:41; Jude 7), punishment (Matt 25:46), destruction (2 Thess 1:9), and judgment (Heb 6:2) are all described as "eternal" and associated with hell. In the parables of Jesus, eternal punishment parallels eternal life (Matt 25:46), and "eternal" must have the same meaning in both phrases. The other view is that the unrighteous are resurrected for judgment, confined to hell, and are there punished and annihilated. They experience conscious punishment in hell, but for a limited period. This view is often construed as "annihilationist."[31] Though

29. Peterson, *Hell on Trial*, 34.

30. Tertullian (c.160–c.240) was an early Christian theologian; Latin name Quintus Septimius Florens Tertullianus. His work includes writings on Christian apologetics, attacks on pagan idolatry, and Gnosticism (see entry in *Oxford English Dictionary*: https://en.oxforddictionaries.com/definition/tertullian).

31. It is directly related to the doctrine of conditional immortality, the idea that a human soul is not immortal unless it is given eternal life. Annihilationism asserts that God

annihilation transpires not at death but after the resurrection and judgment), "conditional immortality is commonly employed to refer to eternal life of the righteous or 'simply conditionalism.'"[32] Our attention now turns to Scripture as much of the proof-texting comes from these teachings about "eternal hell."

Luke 16:19-31

Peterson argues that "care should be taken, what we deduce from this parable, things that God did not intended."[33] Knoch suggests, "The cambric of the Priest and the purple of the king in the rich man's garment indicate Israel as the royal priesthood. His merry times are due to Israel special blessings. The Pharisees looked down upon sinners and publicans and gave them a place like that of Lazarus, outsider with the dogs even as the prodigal was afar off with the swine. they had little more than the unclean aliens who were called curs (wild dogs) by the religious Jews."[34] Fudge does not agree with Knoch's hypothesis; he argues that "This parable so clearly teaches the orthodox doctrine of eternal punishment that the opponents are hard pressed to know what to do with it."[35] However, is Fudge's line of thinking correct, is Knoch incorrect, and did rabbinical Jews read the Scriptures in the same vein as their evangelical Western counterparts? Peterson thinks this is the case; in his view the parable seeks to understand how we deal with people so as to avoid eternal hell.[36] Fudge further argues

---

will eventually destroy the wicked, leaving only the righteous to live on in immortality. Some annihilationists (e.g. Seventh-day Adventists) believe God's love is scripturally described as an all-consuming fire and that sinful creatures cannot exist in God's presence. Thus those who elect to reject salvation through their free will are eternally destroyed because of the inherent incompatibility of sin with God's holy character. Seventh-day Adventists posit that living in eternal hell is a false doctrine of pagan origin, as the wicked will perish, as the Bible says, in the lake of fire. Jehovah's Witnesses believe that there can be no punishment after death because the dead cease to exist.

32. Rosner et al., *New Dictionary of Biblical Theology*, 543–44.

33. "For example, it is tempting to teach that fates are sealed at death because verse 26 says that "great chaise has been fixed" that prohibits movement in either direction. This is indeed a biblical truth, but what was Jesus intending to teach here" (Peterson, *Hell on Trial*, 66).

34. Knoch, *Rich Man and Lazarus*, 122.

35. "The plot of the parable, the reversal of earthly fortunes after deaths a familiar unpopular Palestine stores of Jesus' time" (Fudge, *Fire That Consumes*, 203).

36. "Lazarus and his fearless neighbor's depict... those who demonstrate by their

"the parable's interpretation must include its context. I agree that context within the framework of a hermeneutical in relation to the life-setting of the text will help the reader. And nothing in the context remotely suggests the final state of the wicked (this is noteworthy indeed), though Jesus does clearly intend to teach several other lessons."[37] Fudge further added that the content of the parable clearly possesses elements of Pharisaical snobbery.[38] Fudge further explained, "Jeremias classes the parable with three other call "double edged" (Matt. 22:1–14, 20:1–16; Luke 15:11–32). In each case Jesus begins with a story familiar to his audience. However having gained their attention and probably their approval or disapproval. He throws in an "epilogue" which contains His real message. The stress is therefore in that second point-intel cases the plight of the five living brothers who are ignoring the Word of God. The parable should not be called The Rich Man and Lazarus but the six brothers."[39] Knoch, however, sees the connection of this parable in a way of parallelism between these fivefold stories.[40] Crockett argued from an unnihilistic perspective and in particular notes that this text in question corresponds to a text in Isaiah 66:24.[41]

---

attitudes to material possessions a proper or improper relationship with God" (Peterson, *Hell on Trial*, 68).

37. Fudge, *Fire That Consumes*, 206.

38. "Jesus teaching warns then against self-justification, that that God knows their hearts and that what men highly value God often detest (14 15). The rich man and Lazarus provide perfect illustrations of this truth" (Fudge, *Fire That Consumes*, 207).

39. Fudge, *Fire That Consumes*, 207.

40. "Lazarus whose name (Hebrew, Helpless) is the antithesis of Pharisaism. There hope was in themselves; who's hope was in God alone. We must be careful, how we interpret the description here of Lazarus conditions. A reference to the opening section of the parable my keep us form missing the true point. In the story of the lost sheep we saw that the ninety-nine "Just persons" were merely just and without need of repentance in their own minds. As the story of the sheep, we have the Pharisees' conception of themselves, so in the story of Lazarus we have the conception of the tribute collectors and sinners whom Christ received. They virtually place themselves outside the bounds of Israel's nation favor. The dog—the accepted type of the Gentile—who comes and licks his sores may tell of the plane to which the tribute collector belonged in the Pharisees' estimation. The dog had no part in the rich man's feast though the bones and scraps were not defined him Lazarus had merely the dog's share of eh rich man's banquet" (Knoch, *Rich Man and Lazarus*, 18, 29).

41. "Mark 9:48 must relate to dead (annihilated) creatures. About 150 BCE the Jewish composer of Judith (16:17) uses Isaiah worm image to say that the wicked will suffer *eternal pain* From the First century on the Fire and worms of Isaiah are commonly placed Hell inflicting pain on the wicked suffer eternally" (Gundry et al., 70).

Doctrine of the Eons

Mark 9:42–48.

In Peterson's comments on this text, he suggests, "Jesus admonishes his listeners to weigh carefully their influence on others. Woe to that person who causes Jesus's followers, described as "little ones-minors" to stumble! The fate of such an evildoer will be worse than being forcibly drowned in the sea (v 42) What could be worse (in his option) than such a terrible death? Being shown in Hell by God himself."[42] The problem with Peterson's reasoning is that in his reading he places medieval theology onto the biblical text through way of inference and supposition. In his view, "Hell in (v 43), is a place where the fire becomes unquenchable."[43] That is, the fires of Hell, according to him, never go out, but these are not in fact the words of Jesus but human reasoning. Fudge quotes St. Augustine's use of the particular passage when he reasoned, "Augustine's observation that reputation and that emphatic warning, coming from the divine lips are enough to make any man tremble . . . The fire however, will be material ad it will torment the bodies of dammed men as well as demon-spirits who are either inner out of a body." Fudge further noted Augustine's lack of exegesis in the first section and it is all the more striking by contrast with the second. He further argued that Augustine's views were apologetic in tone in justifying the punishment of Hell. "Gehanna the Valley of Hinnom just below Jerusalem, must not confounded wither lake of fire, or Tartarus, our unseen commonly called "hell" or Hades. It is the fire and worms are quite literal as can be, for the city offal was burned there. No living beings were cast into the incinerator. It is the worms which feed on the carcasses of criminals, who do not die. The fire was kept during at all times. This will be the place where bodies of executed malefactors-criminals be cast during the kingdom era."[44] The notion of Peterson is not altogether clear as he highlights this as a vivid picture of "eternal Punishment" but the word "eternal" is not in the text.

---

42. "In light of the disastrous wages of sin, Jesus drastic action. Rather than indulge in sin, his listener must perform "spiritual surgery on their lives (cvv 43, 45, 47). It is better to "cut off" the offending hand or foot and to "pluck our" the transgression eye to be whole but to go to hell! keeping with Palestinian custom Jesus does not "refer to an abstract activity but to specific member of the body which is responsible for that" (Peterson, *Hell on Trial*, 62).

43. "Every mighty forest fires, which may burn for weeks, eventually burn out. Hellfire, however, is inextinguishable. It is unwise to press Jesus' words concerning fires of hell by asking about the temperature of the flames, for example. His main point is crystal clear: the pains of hell last forever" (Peterson, *Hell on Trial*, 63).

44. Knoch, *Problem of Evil*, 74; and Fudge, *Fire That Consumes*, 66.

Pinnock argues "those who are cast into *Gehanna*, Jesus says "Their worms do not die, and the fire is not quenched.""" Some assume that this text implies everlasting conscious suffering. However, it does not imply it if you link its corresponding text with imagery of Isaiah 66:4 from which the phrase is drawn. Fudge agrees with Pinnock, noting "that the language of the text is in fact figurative, typical prophetic symbolism."[45] Yet Fudge takes an annihilationist view on this text which Peterson disagrees with. He tabulated that "the worm that does not dies is eternal punishment, he postulated that Fudge is reading a back trajectory of the Isaiah an text into the New Testament quotation by Jesus."[46] Peterson contradicts his own thesis by suggesting "the living Christ still uses his messages of hell to save sinners today."[47] I think he means to scare sinners today. In what sense does Peterson's ontology provide the basis for a loving Savior? And Fudge's view, though less extreme, gives no hope for a postmortem eschatological soteriology. Pinnock highlights an all-important point: he sees these as symbols that are very typical of the prophetic genre. However, to what extent does the image extend, and how far do we stretch these text into areas that are not there? Fudge may have pulled reference as an allusion, but Jesus does not speak of the Isaiah text as a fulfillment of what he said, rather he uses a method of hypotaxis.[48] This is not unusual, as the Apostle Paul in later revelation employs the same approach. We cannot speak of a "loving God" who shows you "Hell" in order to save you; this is divisive and deceptive in its epistemology. This goes against the very grain of the nature and character of God, who clearly demonstrates in the biblical revelation that He is Love. Archibald T. Robertson, in engaging with this text, comments that it implies eternal punishment; he further presents the issues, but what he means in a roundabout way is that the "worms" in both texts implies "eternal punishment." The Goodspeed translation clearly expresses the thought

---

45. "God executes judgment "with fire and His sword." (v 16) When the visitation has ended, "many will be throes slain by the Lord (V16b). The wicked "meet there end together (v 17)The righteous and the descendants endure forever (v 22) All mankind" comes to worship God (v 23)—the wicked are no more" (Fudge, *Fire That Consumes*, 110–11).

46. In fact, Jesus sharpens Isaiah's preview of hell when He says that it is a place where the "worms does not die" What Isaiah saw dimly from after Jesus broadcast to all who will hear-hell has no end" (Peterson, *Hell on Trial*, 63–64).

47. Peterson, *Hell on Trial*, 64.

48. "The arrangement of words, phrases, or clauses interns of coordinate and subordinate relationships; the style of writing clearly reflects logical, causal, or temporal relationships" (Tate, *Handbook for Biblical Interpretation*, 204–6).

Doctrine of the Eons

in the Greek: "*You might better enter upon life crippled, than be thrown With both hands and feet into a pit. And your eye makes you fall, tear it out. You might better get into the Kingdom of God with only one eye than with both eyes into a pit, where worm that feeds upon never dies and the fire not never put out.*" Coltfelter argues, "He was evoking the image of an accursed evil-smelling incineration dump crawling with maggots." Coltfelter further argues that the imagery demonstrates the final state of the lost, but he sought to demonstrate that all the images that we have discovered in this context are in fact metaphorical.[49] Although Coltfelter contradicts my earlier point, he however tabulated a key point that is worth noting; in spite of the argument for eternal punishment, he places the "Judgment seat of Christ" and the "Glory Throne" and "White Throne" all together as one general judgment. Thus he sees judgment as a basis of works, but he does not make a distinction between the initiated and the uninitiated. He is not particularly clear, but he makes the assumption for the wicked to be judged. Burnfield, however, does not agree with Clotfelter or Peterson when he argues "that it is not possible to believe that the fires will burn eternally."[50] Burnfield further suggests that "Unquenchable fire in Scripture often signify the fire's immunity from human efforts to extinguish it."[51] This could be a plausible way of understanding it. However, Burnfield tabulated that punishment does not mean eternal, and he employs two text from Jeremiah to clarify his hypothesis.[52] Ramelli and Konstan agreed with Burnfield, who postulated

---

49. "All of these images—a lake of fire, a blazing fire, a place of utter darkness, an incineration dump have an absolute quality above them, in that it difficult to imagine gradations of offerings of those tormented in these ways. Being cast into a lake of burning duller would produce agony in every nerve ending; being banished to blackness darkness would isolate and Terrify every soul so treated. Yet the Bible makes it clear that judgment is according to our deeds (2 Cor 5:10), and Jesus teaches that punishment will be meted out in accordance with degree of one's knowledge of the will of God (Luke 12:47–48; Matt 11:22–24; Rom 2:12) This provides another excellent reason for us to interpret the images of hell as primary metaphorical rather than literal. Hell will be terrible for all who end up there, but will be more or less terrible depending on the kind of lives they have lived in this world God's judgment will be just, and his punishment will be perfectly propionate to our sins. According to Edwards, "The dammed in hell would give the to have the number of their sins one less" (Coltfelter, *Sinners in the Hands of a Good God*, 88).

50. "Peterson takes an utraliteral view of the obviously figurative passage to support his belief in eternal punishment. He pouts is that because worms never die and the fires are continually burning—contrast to what we see happen in nature—eternal punishment is the lesson" (Burnfield, *Patristic Universalism*, 150).

51. Burnfield, *Patristic Universalism*, 150.

52. Jer 7:20, 31:38–40.

that "Gehanna is glossed for those who do not do Hebrew semantics, as "inextinguishable fire", but this, rather than pointing to the eternal duration of the fire, may be simply of differentiating it from the fire of the world, which can be put out: the other fire no human being can extinguish."[53] Talbott argues that "the teaching of universal reconciliation is logically consistent with purgatorial suffering . . . furthermore the parable of the Rich Man and Lazarus is a clear Indication that, according to Jesus In any event, the fate of the wicked is sealed forever as the moment of their physical death, and sealed in a way that exempts any future redemptive hope."[54] Talbott provides a plausible interpretative argument. "The cross had already bridge the relevant chasm, so that the rich man and Lazarus are now living harmoniously in a context of love repentance and forgiveness . . . According to this parable of the Rich Man and Lazarus, even if we take its details more true to life than we ought in the case of a parables, excludes the notion that this rich man will discover his shalom and reconciliation in the end."[55] Walls agrees with Talbot, however, he further opines, "despite the rich man's misery, he appears more concerned to justify himself than to truly repent and sincerely throw himself on God's mercy. In spite of the initial request is for relief from pain, his next request is for Lazarus to be sent to his brothers to warn them so they can escape his fate . . . Hell is indeed a place of misery but not unbearable misery. This is the reason for it to be freely chosen forever as one's eternal destiny."[56] There is a contradiction in Wall's argument: people do not choose to go to "Hell" because it has more or less degrees of pain—this is not in keeping with logical thought. Furthermore, Snodgrass

---

53. Ramelli and Konstan, 126.

54. "This parable describes a rich man who completely ignores the plight of a poor man name Lazarus whom he see daily buying at his gate "covered with sores" and desperately hungry. When Lazarus dies, he finds himself in Hades being tormented in flames for sinful neglect of Lazarus. But when the rich man begs Abraham to send Lazarus (irony of ironies) to bring some real to his own boring tongue with a drop of water, Abraham reminds him of his own neglect of Lazarus during there early lives and the makes the following declaration:(V 26)" (Talbott, *Inescapable Love of God* (1999), 86, 87).

55. Talbott, *Inescapable Love of God* (1999), 88.

56. Walls, *Heaven, Hell and Purgatory*, 83–84.

posits, "the parable divided into three parts not two."[57] Knoch[58] coined it "The four two-edged": "the point of the parable is to do with the reversal of fortunes in life."[59] G. Campbell-Morgan argues "Jesus, used this narrative parabolically; there can be no doubt whatever it then should be conferred this story as parabolic, whether from actual life, or an imaginary picture."[60] Both the reveals of fortunes of rich and poor and the motif of the revelation of the fate of the dead, sometimes even by resuscitation, fit the genre of stories of travel to the realm of the dead. Therefore the mere mention of the resurrection and disbelief do not automatically point to Jesus's resurrection, or show that verses 27–31 are secondary any more than the description of the prodigal as dead and living. The fundamental focus of the parable is somewhat pedantic, for all the components are necessary; first we see at least in the two themes of the parable—judgment for the use of wealth and the sufficiency of the Scriptures—are equally important. So much attention is drawn to the rich man and Lazarus that the first part of the parable cannot be accorded secondary status. If we can presume that this meaning was understood by the hearers of the parables, then it signifies that this meaning was God's identification with the poor and does not permit the hearer to think Lazarus is cursed because of his condition. He is poor and miserable, but God is still on his side.[61] Consequently, Snodgrass further highlights: "One must resist the notion that the parable presupposes that Lazarus has faith or any moral advantage. That is not the concern

57. "It is provocative, by the way that Jesus gave the poor man a name, Lazarus, and the rich man none. The opposite might have been culturally expected—either both should have been anonymous or it one was named, then it should have been the rich man.IN fact, later tradition, in an attempt to sole this inequality, takes the term on the Latin translation of the New Testament *dives* which basically means "rich man and turns turn into a proper noun, "Dives". The parable is simply a reverse of fortunes" (Crossen, *Power of Parable*, 94).

58. "We must be consistent in our interpretation. Luke 15–16 we have a five-fold parable of the Prodigal Son correspond with the Rich Man and Lazarus" (Knoch, *Rich Man and Lazarus*, 4).

59. "As the first part is drawn from well known folk-material, the emphasis lies on the fresh part that Jesus added on the epilogue lies o the fresh part that Jesus added-on he second point. This means that Jesus does not want to comment on social problems, or intend to give teaching about life after death-he tells the parable to warn people like the rich man and his brothers of the impending fate. It should not be called the parable of "Rich man and Lazarus, but the parable of the Six Brothers" (Jeremias, *Rediscovering the Parables*, 149).

60. Morgan, *Parables and Metaphors of our Lord*, 198.

61. Snodgrass, *Stories with Intent*, 429.

of the parable, we must bear in mind that parables are vignettes, not systems, and certainly not systematic theologies. This is not the literal discretion of how judgment will take place."[62]

With this text in mind, it is a clear example from the divergent views from different sources that we have perused; we have parleyed over the prevailing evangelical thinking and from both sides of the chasm it is clear that this text should not be used as a proof text to buttress endless torment. However, based on the evidence weighed, I am in favor of the views of Fudge, Pinnock, and Coltfelter, as they present a pursuable argument that is textually appropriate to the question at hand; also they are of a dispensational bent like Knoch, who presents the argument in light of the literary genre of the text itself. I think this text, correlated to the Isaiah text, clearly demonstrates that during the Millenium Kingdom eon, there will be criminals whose corpses will be thrown into the refuge dump, where the worm dies not and the fire does not go out, because it is the refuse dump (so-called hell fire) of the city. Robertson's line of thinking is correct, but he then turns his argument into his own view on "eternal torment" as being the interpretation for undying maggots. There are no metaphors for maggots in the text. Yet this is his view, and it is is agreed with by many evangelical scholars.

Consequently, as Talbott posits "so far we have no ground for a doctrine of everlasting punishment, in the words of Jesus, as recorded in either the parable of the Sheep and the Goats or the parable of the Rich Man and Lazarus."[63] I agree with Talbott's contestation. For this reason, we note that the entire argument is couched in symbolic language, bearing in mind that this is a parable unlike any other parable and it is not to be taken literally. As Snodgrass contends, "parables are fictional deceptions taken from everyday life. However, they do not necessarily portray everyday events. Quite the contrary, while some are realistic some are not. A few draw on historical events, but they do not depict true stories. Because of hyperbole and elements of surprise or improbability, parables are *pseudo—realistic* and have elements that shock."[64] Are there any conclusive arguments to this debate? At this point in time, the debate rages on with little sign of abating. There-

---

62. Snodgrass, *Stories with Intent*, 429.

63. Talbott, *Inescapable Love of God* (2014), 88.

64. "They are told to create interest and numerous schemes are employed to draw hears in and compel dealing with issues also used soliloquy (especially in Luke), dialogue, exaggeration and concrete details . . ." (Snodgrass, *Stories with Intent*, 18).

fore we contend that our embedded views that we seek to hold on to require more self-searching, investigative introspection, and revisiting of our assumptions; in so doing, we may encounter some interesting things. Do not look at the surface of things but dig deeper and engage critically with our assumptions. Robertson's *Word Pictures of the New Testament* agrees with my point.[65]

The intention of this section was to engage with a number of texts, allowing us to engage within the literary genre and exegetically engaging with wider reading sources. In spite of my own limited assumptions, in my choice of biblical texts, we sought to provide the rationale for my assumption, in viewing the biblical text the way that I do. Furthermore I acknowledge that my own assumptions are not often greeted with glee within the prism of my own evangelical wing of my own theological praxis. Snodgrass's arguments sought to provide a reasonable rationale that this is a parable and that we should not make it into a systematic theological doctrine; I think that this has fallen on deaf ears. As Peterson, Walls, and others have committed that same exegetical fallacy of proof text in their assumptions about the text. Jersak argued, "Medieval visionaries and modern evangelicals historically have a commitment to belief in a liberalized lake of fire as a crux of biblical faithfulness; he further contends that visionary experiences are often conflated between "literal" and the "real" in a way that does not do justice to the biblical text."[66] We maintain that this was one of the many other so-called retributive texts which we will engage when we speak of soteriology in the next part. We will look at salvation as praxis within the confine of universal salvation. Did the readers of the Old and New Testament misunderstand the love of God? Is the love of God the pivotal point for salvation, and if yes, how so? We will seek to answer these questions.

---

65. "Not Hades, but Gehenna The Vally Hinnom has desecrated been desecrated by the sacrifices of children to Moloch so that as an accursed place it was used for the city garbage where worms gnawed and fires burned. It is thus a video picture of eternal punishment" (Robertson, *Word Pictures*, 346).

66. Jersak, *Her Gates Will Never Be Shut*, 153–54.

13

Universal Salvation as Praxis

WHAT IS UNIVERSAL SALVATION and how best can we explain it as praxis? Universal salvation is the doctrine that teaches that all mankind will be saved (1 Tim 2:4, 4:10). With this in mind, it does not mean that all humanity will go to heaven. What it does mean is that God will bring about salvation of all throughout the course of the eons. This doctrine is at odds with current Western thought. I contend that the teaching of universal salvation is comparable to the basic meaning of the word "salvation" as expostulated within Western thought.

The focus that we want to bring to the fore is salvation from the standard that is commonly accepted in Western thought. We will not look at it from the Hebrew Scriptures but rather we will look at the definition of salvation from a New Testament standpoint. *Sōzō* ("save," "keep from harm" "rescue," "heal," or to "liberate") occurs 106 times and its compound *diasōzō* nine times. At times, "save" involves some individual being delivered from physical danger. Thus Paul is rescued from numerous perils, including shipwreck, on the way to Rome.[1]

In a number of ways human beings serve as agents of salvation. Through an encounter with the risen Lord (1 Cor 9:1; 15:8) which he describes as "a revelation of Jesus Christ" (Gal 1:12), Paul knows that he has been called to proclaim God's Son "among the Gentiles," (Gal 1:16). He is "eager" to visit Rome and preach "the Gospel" which is "the power of

---

1. Acts 23:24, 27:20; 31, 34, 43, 45; 28:1, 4; see Freedman et al., *Anchor Bible Series*, 910.

Doctrine of the Eons

God for salvation for all of the faith of Jesus Christ" (Rom 1:15-16, 1 Cor 1:18; 15:1—2). Paul's missionary journey helped to provide salvation for everyone (Rom 11:14).

"In the main Pauline corpus, the futurity of salvation is especially prominent. Apropos of the final destiny of Israel, Paul passes from negative question from Isaiah ("Through the number of Sons of Israel be saved as the sand of the sea, only a remnant of them will be saved" (Rom 9:27). To maintain, on the authority of the same prophets, said that," all Israel will be saved." (Rom 11:26) In his own case Paul is sure that sufferings will bring his "deliverance" (Phil 1:19). He informs the Philippians to look to the future." Paul clearly appreciates the role of God's free and loving initiative in effecting human salvation: "God shows his love for us in that while we were yet sinners Christ dies for us . . ."[2]

"During the history of the church in the New Testament times the doctrine of Salvation has constantly been in danger of misunderstanding and corruption. Most commonly, salvation has been thought of something that people must earn or merit by doing actions that please God in order to win favor. At the Protestant Reformation, the Protestant insisted that the doctrine of justification by faith is the indication of whether the church is standing or falling from the truth of the Gospel. They realized that Salvation is the gift of God and that the church must not usurp his place in declaring who can be saved, even if it is true that the church is appointed to proclaim the gospel. Salvation has sometimes been operated from the person of Jesus who's is then regarded as little more than a teacher of morality; the recognition that God was in Christ to reconcile sinful world to himself has been lost, and salvation has been thought of as exclusively deliverance from ignorance of God and not also as cleansing from sin and its guilt."[3] The scope of salvation always had been a matter of dispute. The Old Testament usage of the terms to express God's action in saving his people from their enemies has been taken as normative, and salvation has been construed as emancipating people from hunger, poverty, and threat of war, so that they may live a whole life in the world; the thought of spiritual salvation has retreated into in the background.[4] McGrath contends that "Salvation is an act in which is placed number of individuals or groups of individuals."[5] I agree with Mc-

---

2. Freedman et al., *Anchor Bible Series*, 912.
3. Wright et al., *New Dictionary of Theology*, 610.
4. Wright et al., *New Dictionary of Theology*, 610.
5. "Salvation is understood to mean "some benefit conferred upon or achieved by

Grath's initials premise, as it still set the tone for "universal salvation" in that it is that act which is conferred on humanity. This makes salvation exclusive as oppose to inclusive. Christianity therefore, as McGrath assumes, is not discrimination or unique in attaching importance to the idea of salvation. The Christian approach to lies in two areas. Initially salvation is construed to be grounded in the life, death, and resurrection of Jesus Christ, and the other is the specific shape of salvation within Christian tradition which is itself formed by Christ.[6] Bloesch argues, "Salvation is a free gift of God, that it cannot be earned or merited by our good merited by our good behavior."[7] Bloesch posits the notion that salvation is not based upon human achievement or any form of meritorious works of human endeavor. This is true, yet others accuse proponents of universal salvation that this is not the case. Furthermore, I contend that salvation is solely a work of God and not the work of man. Bloesch disagrees. He proposes that salvation is a paradox in the sense that "it eludes rational comprehension. That laps into synergism and monogerigism can be accounted for by the ever-recurring attempts to resolve the paradox of salvation into a rationally understandable formula."[8] For Bloesch, salvation should perceived as an act of God and man; this is a synergistic approach. This would then make man coequal or partner in the salvific process. The problem with human freedom contributing to salvation is that it places human beings as the captain of their ship and masters of their fate. For this reason, we are not suggesting that those who receive salvation do not have a choice; however, we should bear in mind that free will is the hallmark of orthodoxy, and it is not believed to be authentic and quintessential. This beliefe has proponents like Alvin Plantinga's work, *God Freedom, and Evil*. This seminal work provides the basis from a philosophical approach to human freedom. "God can create free creatures, but he cannot cause or determine them to do only what is right. For if he does so, then they aren't significantly free after all, they do not do what is right

---

members of a community, whether individually or corporately." All religions offer "salvation." However, this is such a verbal statement that is devoid of significant theological value" (McGrath, *Christian Theology*, 327).

6. McGrath, *Christian Theology*, 327.

7. "Good works are not good enough to satisfy the stringent requirements of God's law. If man is to be saved he must be pardoned on the basses of the perfect righteousness of the Son of God who condescended to stand in man's place" Bloesch, *Essentials of Evangelical Theology*, 181.

8. Bloesch, *Essentials of Evangelical Theology*, 201.

Doctrine of the Eons

freely."[9] Peterson shares the view of Plantinga, but he goes a step further like Bloesch, who takes a synergistic view of salvation.[10] Peterson further contends, "The ultimate purpose of Salvation is complete glorification and complete sanctification in the presence of God on the renewed earth. True freedom will be perfected only after the resurrection of the dead."[11] Knoch disagrees with this hypothesis when he insists "The human will is dual in its source. It is the product of heredity and environment each of these is an inextricable complex composite which none can analyses, much less control. Why is it the will of men to Sin? Because is part of their inheritance. We cannot argue they are free to sin, for them some might escape. Has any person the choice of their ethnic origin, their respective nationality or the place of their birth? Yet what important factors these are in every act of one's life? Can we think of volition in a single matter which is not affected by factors which one has not the remotest control? What is meant by Freedom of Will is correspondence between heredity and environment, were does the will come from? Do people create it out of a vacuum. Or Imagine our volition were planted by us from our own hands, or that they have been conjured forth by us from the void of vacuity. So that our will arises without root, and flourishes without soil, water or air, is sheer imbecility. Our wills to a large extent by our determine by our ancestors especially one named Adam."[12] Talbott contends, "I perform a given action *freely* in the relevant sense only if it is within my power, at the time of acting, not to perform it; and it is within my power, at the time of acting, not to perform a given action only if, initially, it is logically possible that I do not perform it and, second, nothing outside of my control causally determines (or necessitates) that I do perform it."[13] In other words, what Talbott proposes is that the argument of freedom limits the omnipotence of God and places God on par with human will, thereby limiting its power to override human choices and intentions. What does God know? Or what does God not know? It is a matter of scholastic opinion to say the least; at the outset, advocates

---

9. Plantinga, *Good, Freedom and Evil*, 30.

10. "God's election of his people for salvation because of election is the book's primary subject. However, to ignore human free will would be inexcusable,. Divine Sovereignty and predestination that flows from it, must viewed alongside human freedom and, and faith in Christ flows from it. Otherwise distortion will result" (Peterson, *Election and Free Will*, 125).

11. Peterson, *Election and Free Will*, 131.

12. Knoch, *Problem of Evil*, 119, 121.

13. Talbott, *Inescapable Love of God* (2014), 175.

Universal Salvation as Praxis

of free will commandeer the word "choice" (and its synonyms) and boldly incorporate the notion of *avoid ability* into the term itself, even though this is actually no part of the meaning of any volitional synonym. Instead it is merely what most Christians believe to be true concerning human choice; this extremely common practice is completely unwarranted and leads to insidious error. For a choice is basically that which is chosen or selected; our option as to whether or not choices are avoidable form no part of the meaning of the word itself and ought not to be forced into it.

Due to the influences from within and without, a person may well change in the next moment from what they are in the present moment; however, any certain moment one's deeds are basically the outworking of the heart (Prov 4:23). They reflect what is presently a choice for them; that is, they constitute the true preference, but they may be excellent or awful.

Though we do what we want according to our own choice, and therefore act voluntarily, we cannot always want what we want. That is, we cannot truly want, in a decisive sense, what we want, in an abstract sense, so long as there are other things that we want more, in a decisive sense, than we want the ideals for which we abstractly long. Even if, abstractly speaking, we prefer the "temporary enjoyment of sin" (Heb 11:25), this is the very message of Romans 7:15–23, as well as that of all perceptive personal observation. It is vital for us to be clear as to these two distinct senses in which the word "want" (or will) is employed.

Due to our self-reliance, pride, impatience, and anger, coupled with our self-assured ethical notions about praise, blame, and judgment, this hypothesis of contrary choice is an extremely attractive one. Then there is the matter of our strong desire, whether acknowledged or not, for independent personal glory. Hence the intention becomes the father to the claim and consequently, the foundation of human ethics.[14] Coram presents

---

14. "Advocates of this position, who ought to be called, "The power of country choice," performer to perpetuate it instead under the innocuous and advantageously ambitious of a respectable-sounding name, and makes those few who are constrained to reject the actual doctrine appear strange extremist, inasmuch as they reject such well-accepted, desirable and seemingly reasonable concept. The advocate of free will actually stands for the position which asserts that human choices are uncased-absolutely devoid of all necessity. And yet they do not realize, nor act lease they refuse to admit the fact, that the denial of causality will bring them any closer to what they what than its advocacy" (Knoch et al., *Unsearchable Riches*, 4).

an augment that is quite illuminating as he seeks to engage the thought against free will; Coram noted that tenants of free will have the propensity to be selfish in their deduction as to what they deem to be choice, in that they perceive freedom and choice as an arbitrary God-given right. Much to the contrary of such dedication, Talbott argues from the position that the Arminian position is fundamentally flawed.[15] No one chooses to go to hell; such is the doctrine of Western thought. However, Knoch argues, "Mankind imagine they are sovereign in the realm of the will and that one can break the resolution—no, not even God. This is childish. They have no greater control over it than the captain of a sailing vessel has over the set of his sails. If they are not determined for this or by the breeze. There are spiritual winds to which mankind bend their wills. They may whistle ever so long, but these spirit forces are beyond their perception and above their control."[16] I agree that this is the very thing that human beings fail to understand; they deduce that such an argument is valued because God does not make humans into robots! To which Plantinga, in his defense of free will, responds: "God can create free creatures, however he can't *cause* or *determine* them to do only what is right. For if He does so, then they aren't significantly free after all; they do not do what is right freely. To create capable of *moral good*, thus, He must create creatures capable of moral evil."[17] Plantinga went a step further by arguing that God created human beings with the capacity to do moral evil as with the ability to create moral good.[18] Peterson called it "freedom of spontaneity."[19]

With this in mind, Peterson is not suggesting that freedom of will is in fact a matter of choice, and not a freedom of will, but rather the ability to freely love God and to worship God in a free environment. This appears contradictory to what Plantinga argues. Furthermore, we note that for

15. "The hypothesis of someone freely rejecting God forever, is deeply incoherent, and therefore logically impossible; even if such a notion were perfectly coherent, a loving God would never allow his loved ones to make such a choice, because he would net er permit them to do irreparable harm to themselves or to others; and the free will theist\'s understanding of hell is, in any case, utterly inconsistent wither New Testament teaching about hell" (Talbott, *Inescapable Love of God* (2014), 170–71).

16. Knoch, *Problem of Evil*, 122.

17. Plantinga, *Good, Freedom and Evil*, 30.

18. Plantinga, *Good, Freedom and Evil*, 30.

19. "God made Adam and Eve for himself, he made to know love, and serve and each other. True freedom to make spontaneous choices; it is also freedom of relationship with God-ability to know, love, serve, enjoy him-and with other human beings" (Peterson, *Election and Free Will*, 126).

Peterson, "Freedom of choice is the ability to make spontaneous choices according to the inclinations of the will."[20] Geisler purports a balanced view. He contends, "God is in control of the universe, he does not force anyone's freedom, however he knows beforehand, what everyone is going to freely do."[21] Geisler holds a simpler view to that of William Lane Craig[22] who contends that God has "Middle Knowledge,"[23] that is, "Means of Salvation."[24] Keathly contends, "This is an imaginative use of perseverance, can this be interpreted that the believer is capable of falling away, (backsliding), even if they do not apostatize? Hypothetically, at least, the elect can apostatizes, yet God, employs middle knowledge, has chosen to actualize a world in which scriptural warnings will operate as a means to keep his children from falling away."[25]

Molina's doctrine of scientia media is called middle knowledge because it stands in the middle of two traditional categories of divine epistemology as handed down by Aquinas: natural and free knowledge. It shares

---

20. Peterson, *Election and Free Will*, 132.

21. "God was free to create or not create, to create free creatures or not create them. Knowingly exactly what would happen in every possible word, would freely chose to create this one to achieve the greatest good. His omniscient for knowledge assumes that it's going to come out of exactly as he know it would" (Geisler, *Chosen But Free*, 19).

22. "God foreknows future free acts, God does foreknows all future events including human choices and actions, but only because not them other are genuinely free" (Craig, *Time and Eternity*, 44).

23. "Middle Knowledge is a form of knowledge first attributed to God by the sixteenth century Jesuit theologian Luis de Molina. It is best explained that God prevocational knowledge of all true counterfactual pf creaturely freedom. This knowledge is seen by projects as the key to understanding the capability of divine providence and creaturely (liberation) freedom). Middle Knowledge is coo construed between natural and free knowledge of God's deliberations regarding the creative process. According to this hypothesis, middle knowledge is like natural knowledge in that is pre volitional, or prior to God's choice to create. This, of course, can be construed that the content of middle knowledge is true independent of God's will independent of God 's will and therefore, He has no control over it. Albeit, its difference to that of natural and fee knowledge, its content is contingent. Middle knowledge proposes that God has knowledge of metaphysically necessary state of affairs via natural knowledge, of what Hew intends to via free knowledge, and in addition, of what free creatures would do if they were instantiated" ("Middle Knowledge." *Internet Encyclopedia of Philosophy*. https://www.iep.utm.edu/middlekn/).

24. "using middle knowledge has chosen to actualize a world in which warnings will operate was means to keep His children from apostasy" (Keathley, *Salvation Sovereignty*, 186).

25. Keathley, *Salvation Sovereignty*, 186.

characteristics of each and in logical order of the divine deliberative process regarding creation. It follows natural knowledge but proceeds through free knowledge.[26] How does this middle knowledge help to provide an eschatological universal salvation for proponents like Craig, Keathley and Geisler, who contend that punishment exists for the ungodly at the end of their life at the great White Throne? They all agree in their view of the all-knowing God, and rightly so they see the sovereignty of God working in and through human actions. What then can God not attain in what He intends? Keathley argues, "The distinctive difference between Calvinism Molinism is that Calvinism views of God as accomplishing His will through his omnipotent power, while Molinism understands God's employment of omniscient through knowledge."[27] Therefore, for God to save all, He knows all, whether it is fact or feeling. It is important that in understanding God's will, it is essential to not only be acquainted with the God of the sacred Scriptures, but the God of all flesh. How we come to this assumption is either through free or natural knowledge, or through middle knowledge or counterfactual argument, as we have defined. The stated fact is, God will have all be saved.[28] The counterfactual argument would be, if God is not a savior, would God be able to save all? The answer would be no! Hence is the counterfactual true. No! If the counterfactual is true, then that which is true as to fact would be false. This would mean that God did not create humans to save them, and that he is powerless to save all, thus all are consigned to death and hell to a particular place in the universe. The notion that God would save all but he cannot is in fact false, yet it is true to those who hold to the assumption of the popular teaching of free will. This in my view puts limits on salvation. For it makes man omnipotent, in the sense that those of mankind who choose can reject the will of God, and have the power of contrary choice. Talbott noted flaws in Craig's deduction of Molina's middle knowledge in relation to free will and his Arminian view of hell.[29] He posits that the idea

---

26. Natural knowledge is part of God's knowledge which He knows by His nature or essence, and since His essence is necessary, so that which is known through it. Free knowledge is that part of God which He knows by His knowledge of His own Will, both what He desires and what He will, in fact, do. Middle knowledge is so named because it comes between natural and free knowledge in God's deliberation regarding the creative process. According to the theory, middle knowledge is like natural knowledge but is pre-vocational, or prior to God's choice to create.

27. Keathley, *Salvation Sovereignty*, 155.

28. See 1Timothy 2:4, 4:10.

29. Luther, *Bondage of the Will*, 78.

UNIVERSAL SALVATION AS PRAXIS

of God expunging people in the resurrection is somewhat extreme to say the least.[30]

Furthermore, Luther takes the Augustinian view of divine Sovereignty, arguing against Erasmus in the work *The Bondage of the Will* and contends, "Free Will, of its own power, cannot do anything but fall, nor avail unto anything but to sin."[31]

Coram argues with Luther's view and argues: "Whether, "determinism" (that is, causality), divine or otherwise, is true or false, we cannot possibly be free either way-that is, in a freewill or contrast choice sense. If we are caused to choose as we do, we cannot help choosing as we do. Thus, if we are not caused to choose as we do, we still cannot help choosing as we do."[32]

What we seek to understand is salvation as praxis. I contend that the argument of free will championed by orthodoxy is human pride wrapped up in hypocrisy, for out of it we make a human being a deity besides the deity. Furthermore, it supports the notion that human beings are in fact responsible for their salvation. Such a notion presents the cross as ineffectual, as its propensity to save is then only as powerful as a mere desire or wish. This makes the redemptive work a facade.

The entire salvific history of humankind is then placed in the hands of mankind. This is the view of the proponents of free will. Hence the contention among those who are of the view that God is sovereign, all-powerful,

---

30. "Hence the redeemed, expunging from their minds any memory that might interfere with their future happiness. In case of those whose entire family is lost, this would be construed. I assume, that God expunges from their minds every memory of parents and family siblings, and I doubt that Craig has any conception of how much of a person's mind that would likely destroy . . . however, Craig is right, of course, about one thing. We can talk of cases in which were shield persons dorm knowledge which would be painful for them and which they do not need to have, and far from doing something immoral, we are, in so sparing them, exemplifying the virtue of mercy. But withholding information for a season in one thing; obliterating part of the mind forever is something else altogether. The latter reduces God's victory over sin to a cruel hoax; his hollow in "victory" consists not in his making things right, but in his concealing form the redeemed just how bad things really are. Though utterly defeated in the end, god, simply conceals from us the enmity of the defeat" (Talbott, *Inescapable Love of God* (2014), 193).

31. Luther, *Bondage of the Will*, 129.

32. What James Coram contends is that "We cannot be free agents, in the ordinary, strong true—responsibility entailing sense, if determinism is true we and our actions are ultimately determined by causes which existed anterior to our own personal existence" (Knoch et al., *Unsearchable Riches*, 4). True enough and this is highly significant for our understanding of what it means for so-called freedom.

and all-knowing, who is not limited to time and space, but controls all, and who is immutable in all His contrivances.

I argue that free will is a human invention that came into being through neo-gnostic ideas formulated through the past four centuries of church history. I posited philosophical views of salvation from Plantanga, Keathley, Craig, and Peterson who hold to a free will argument essentially have good arguments in view of free will; however, such views are like inanimate objects contending with the maker, "Why do you make me thus?" An ancient proverb states: A man held his hand up in the city square, and contended, "If there is a God, let him put my hand down." This man was bald and very sensitive in that area. A fly came and landed on his bald pate. The fly began tickling his bald head, and down came the hand to swat the fly. The moral of the story is that God answers a fool by his own folly.

I do not agree with Knoch, who highlighted the fact that we are unable to determine our racial ethnicity, nor are we able to determine or choose the air we breathe, or the time of death—we are unable to put it off another day. The quest for endless life is an ongoing scientific debate that has eluded them for eons. The matter is entirely in the hand of the Supreme Deity. I propose to demonstrate in my deduction that free will is not an enactment for salvation nor does it serve as a precursor for it either. Neither does it serve as a recquisite to *eonian* life in the future. I contend that salvation is an act of God and not a part of man; however I do view the notion that salvation has nothing to do with mankind, though it concerns mankind. It is the sovereign will of God to save all. It is his perogative. The work of the cross provides the solution to mankind's ills, and it is this work of redemption which poses a number of socialistic trajectories contrary to the assumption of the verb "save," the noun "salvation," and so on. What I mean by this, from the standpoint of a postmodernist who would deconstruct this narrative, is that such a notion is subjective and relative to one's assumption. Furthermore, the notion that an invisible God could send his Son to die for mankind is nonsense to the atheist. How then can my assumption be proven and watertight when the evidence is not all that apparent? Salvation, like many other biblical terms, is now redundant in a secular, liberal society that is more concerned with the salvation of cats and dogs than the saving of souls. Then there are the issues of race and culture. The salvation posited to people who are non-European has been problematic as I will discuss in the future in more detail. Initially, when we see salvation from the lens of our hermeneutics, I ask, who and what do we see? We do not want to lose the essence of my argument in presenting salvation as universal and that it affects all people regardless of their race. This brings me to the notion of justification. Will God justify all mankind, in spite of our imperfections? Will God justify all mankind and bring about righteousness to all human beings? Will He address the poor, the oppressed, and the margins of society?

All these questions would take another book to explain in more detail, as this is not the project of this work, but this merely highlights some of the poignant facts that are visible in our world today. Will God redress the injustice perpetuated against all darker peoples on the planet Earth is another eschatological question that requires more forensic answers than I will address in this work. Nevertheless we do not want to lose sight of the intention of this book as we seek to engage on universal salvation as praxis. I wish to draw your attention to Talbott's work on *The Inescapable Love of God* where he contends from within the Pauline corpus, "Adam-will receive "justification and life" and will therefore be reconciled to God in the end. (Romans 5:18) Yet our text is, of course, a single sentence, lifted from the context, and see can hardly determine accurately the meaning of the sentence apart from the context in which it occurs. So let us know ask, is their good reasons, either in the immediate context of our text or in the wider context, of Paul's thought as a whole, for believing that Paul did not intend to say what his sentence, taken in isolation, appears to say? I do not think many would agree."33 Knoch posits that justification is the grounds in which God brings about peace and reconciliation.34 Therefore, justification—which is a forensic term in my view—is the notion that mankind is brought before the bar of God and are vindicated because of the vicarious sacrificial atonement on the cross, that is, the accomplished work of Christ on the cross. This is the grounds for justification. Jan Bonda, in his work *The One Purpose of God,* contends: "Adam was called to conquer those powers—to be a blessing for creation. However he failed. Through disobedience he brought the rule of death over all. The new Adam God

---

33. "So then as through one transgression there resulted condemnation to all men, even so through the one act of righteousness there resulted justification of life to all men (5:18) How would we understand such an assertion? To all appurtenances, Paul intensifies one "all"—that is, all human beings—and makes two distinct but parallel statements about that one "all" and the appearance the second of theses statements implies that all human beings shall receive "Justification and life"" (Talbott, *Inescapable Love of God* (1999), 56–57).

34. Knoch, *Concordant Commentary,* 234.

has given is, though his obedience, conqueror of sin and death."³⁵ Bonda noted the problem of this text is that modern exegetes would not see the second "all" as universal, but only believers. He further highlighted the fact that early Reformed exegetes did not see a problem with the parallel statement of the first "all" and the second "all."³⁶ This problem is clearly exhibited by Wright: he does not see justification as being made right with God, nor does he view that it means one has been declared righteous.³⁷ For Wright, justification is misunderstood and the notion that God declares an individual righteousness is in fact a medieval trajectory read back into the biblical text from Reformed theological tradition. So what does Wright mean by this? Wright overlooks the word "all"—rather he seeks to expunge neo-Reformed exegetical approach to the text. For Wright, he sought to exegetically engage the larger context of this particular passage rather than isolating this text from the broader context; Wright posits that the larger context of chapters 5–8 was far more important.³⁸ Nonetheless, I do not think that he sees the universality of the word "justification" for all, leading to reconciliation, and that the word *ta panta* ("the all") is the first and the second is universal in the fullest sense of the word.

Bonda argued that ""verse 18 refers to "all" whereas verse 19 refers to "many" or more precisely, "the many." This word does not imply restrictions:

35. Bonda, *One Purpose of God*, 103.

36. "If the exegesis is correct, it is not true that Christ, through his obedience, more than compensates for the havoc wreaked by the first human disobedience. If Paul writes "much more" it surely must be understood in terms of much more grace, but much more grace for fewer people. Paul's omission of "far fewer people' his simply due to the fact that it was self-evident for and the church that it affected far fewer people. Thus we arrive at an explanation that harmonizes with pessimism of our tradition" (Bonda, *One Purpose of God*, 105).

37. "Justification can't mean 'being made righteous,' as though God pumps a little bit of moral virtue whole. No, Paul replies you've missed the point; haven't gone far enough in eliminating the last traces of mediaeval misunderstanding. 'Righteousness' means that status that you posses as a result of the judge's verdict. For the defendant in the law court standing in the community as a result of the judge's pronouncement.' Imputed righteousness ' is a Reformation answer to a medieval question" (Wright et al., *New Dictionary of Theology*, 187).

38. "Paul had in mind a constant frame of thought in which (a) a judicial event takes place, consisting of (b)the righteous act of Jesus, also designated as his 'obedience,' and referring to the same event as his 'faithfulness,' in other words, his death (3:24–6; 5, 6–10), as a result of which (c) human beings are declared to be in the right, now enjoying the status of 'righteousness' as a result of the verdict which God has announced ' (*dikaiōma*) and God's free gift, so that (d) they might inherit 'the age to come' and not only inherit it but also share Christ reign within it" (Wright et al., *New Dictionary of Theology*, 200–1).

UNIVERSAL SALVATION AS PRAXIS

Many people, but not all. Paul weakens what he said in verse 18, where he emphasized that *all* will be justified. We come across the same formula in verse 12 and verse 15. First of all, death has spread to all, second, the many die through Adam's trespass. Obviously, in the latter case no one is excluded from the "many." Paul uses the word "many" to indicate the extension of the "all" mentioned in verse 18; all people who have ever lived and have died on the earth and all who are yet to follow—the great multitudes that no one can number."[39] Here we can see that Bonda contends the universality of those few passages. Hence Bonda posits the view that I agree with, for he presents the notion that the "many" is equivalent to the "all" of the part of the text, equating to the universality of the part of the many in the latter half of the text. Barth noted, "As the consequence of the righteousness of Christ there comes—justification of life—to all men. Here is the negation of all negation, the death of all death, the breaking down of limitations, the rendering asunder of all fetters, the clothing of all men with their habitation which is from heaven (2 Cor 5:2) For all men death is swallowed up by victory (1 Cor 15:55) and morality is up by life (2 Cor 5:4). All are renewed and clothed with righteousness, and are become a new subject, and are therefore set at freedom and placed under the affection of God."[40] From Barth's own dialectical logic, we can deduce that what he means by this is the negation of the first act (Adam), but is also about another negation (Christ), for the nullifying of death brings about the accomplished victory; all will be made "righteous" as Talbott originally elucidated.

Thus, we see the idea that the context determines the meaning of the text, as Wright seeks to do by eliminating the tradition of patristical reading of the text. Yet ignoring the universality of the text, the all and the many are both equal in the text; universal justification is for all and will be accomplished at the consummation of the eons. How this pans out is not altogether clear without further explaining how humanity can be found in Adam. Knoch's work *All in All* provides some insight to this perplexing question; he contends, "When Adam sinned we were effectively in him. All that we are has come to us, that it through our DNA, so it must have been at least latent in him first—sin that is."[41]

---

39. Bonda, *One Purpose of God*, 106.

40. Barth, *Epistle to the Romans*, 182.

41. "The investigation promoted by the theory of evolution have demonstrated that no living thing transmits anything permanent form its environment or experiences. All come to it tough hereditary, therefore all we see is the development—process of potentialities which were given to the prime member of each species at its beginning. The entire human race was created in Adam as the prime In a very real sense all mankind sinned in

113

Therefore, if we take into consideration the consequences of the act of disobedience, we see the salvation plan Knoch further notes as this: "Christ sacrifice surpasses Adam's act in its qualitative value, so much more will be the measure of its effects over those of Adam's infringement."[42] This is what I think Barth is suggesting when speaking of the double negation, in that the qualitative aspect is exclusive and its result is today's consequence.

Justification, therefore, is the resultant work of the cross (Rom 5:1). It is God that justifies the sinner and this is done through the vicarious sacrificial redemptive atonement. Furthermore, this historical act provides the metaphor for salvation of all human beings. Justification is the grounds in which God will bring about righteousness to all human beings. This statement requires further clarification! Sin was the judge at the cross period. It brought about the resultant act of God, in that He in turn made a decision to put an end to sin at the cross. Its consequence is death. As a result of this, God was justified in this one single act, resulting in justification and life; God declared the one who is of the faith of Jesus Christ (*ton ece pistes Iesou*) to be right and justified (Rom 3:26). What this means in a roundabout way, is that God is right in justifying the believer by the faith of Jesus Christ.[43] R.T Kendall is right: Jesus's own righteousness is imparted to us.[44]

Salvation as praxis is a formula thatdoes not negate judgment or remedial punishment in the final analysis, yet it is in Christ that justification will be manifested.

I sought to engage the notion that justification is one of the formulas of salvation by demonstrating its universal ramification; I sought to create tension by critically examining the prevailing view of justification and the way it is read in tradition and in context.

I do not think that tradition and its reading of Romans 5 is altogether correct, as the Reformers put limits to the word "all" to all those who are

---

him. It is impossible to be of his race and not partake of the penalty of his act. In Adam all are dying, not though, but in. In order to realize and appreciate what Christ is to creation, we will employ Adam, as a way of illustration The weakness of the parallel is the weakness lies in Adams failure. To strengthen it we purpose to relieve Adam temporally of the disabilities brought about by sin, so that we can see more clearly what Christ would be, in his place, and what is Christ, is His higher and earlier position" [quote slightly modified] (Knoch, *All in All*, 102).

42. Knoch, *All in All*, 105.

43. Kendall, *Once Saved Always Saved*, 51.

44. Kendall, *Once Saved Always Saved*, 51.

currently saved, ignoring the universal aspect of the words "all" and "many" and the synonymous parallelism, so as to fit the context.

Wright suggests otherwise. He posits that a larger contextual reading should read within the framework of a Jewish rabbinical lens of the text. That is what exactly Barclay had in mind,[45] by pointing to a reader's response exegetical task. Wright used a judicial law court scene to frame his argument, and while we have little knowledge of first-century courtroom proceedings, yet it is this method—called the punctilios approach—that has flung the door open for a barney on both sides of the Atlantic as to what Paul really said. Wright posits an argument that is well worth tabulating. His work is limited, yet in the limits of his arguments, in my view, is his inability to engage with the universality which he denied in this text. Barclay rightly contends that "Just as all men were involved in Adam's sin, all men are involved In Jesus's perfect goodness."[46] Even this is a good starting point; however, Barclay only sees mankind in the real sense only associated with Adam, so he posits the idea that in a real sense we are in Adam; this is exactly what Knoch said, which I agree with as well. Presenting the argument about the resultant historical act of justification is eschatologically true in the same sense. This is my opinion on the argument.

This brings me to the second point of salvation as praxis, which is reconciliation. I felt that as I engaged with the idea of salvation as praxis, I found myself asking, how does the signified word "salvation" bring about reconciliation? What does reconciliation mean? What I intend to discuss is how salvation is an act of God bringing about conciliation and then eventually reconciliation. What is its consequence, Conciliation-Reconciliation?

Furthermore, I will contend in this section of this chapter that the word conciliation is a lower form of reconciliation, and I will demonstrate that the reconciliation is a signifier to that which brings peace between God and his estranged creatures.

---

45. "The passage ought to be given what is called the realistic interpretation, namely treaty, because of the solidarity of the human race, all mankind actually sinned in Adam. this idea was not strange to Jew; it was the actual belief of the Jewish thinkers. the writer of 2*Esdras* is quite apparent about it "A gain of evil was won in the heart of Adam from the beginning and how much wickedness has it brought forth unto this time; and how shall it yet bring forth till the time of the threshing come" (4:30) The second basic idea is intimately connected with I this Paul's argument Death is the consequence of sin. It was the Jewish belief that, if Adam had not sinned, man would have been immortal. Sirach (2:23)" (Barclay, *Daily Study Bible*, 80).

46. Barclay, *Daily Study Bible*, 80.

Doctrine of the Eons

Conciliation is a new word in theology, yet in the Greek, this is not the case. The actual word form of the verb (*katatallosso*) is an estrangement on one side only.[47] It is the act of one person who wins the favor of the offending party. It is the act in which the peacemaker offers peace to the offender who is hostile in their estrangement towards the peacemaker. The positive aspect to this argument is that the offending party can accept the offer of peace unilaterally, thereby providing the room for mutual reconciliation. This is ideally the notion of what Paul argues in 2 Corinthians 5:18–19. This has been missed by evangelicals who have mistranslated this word by using the word "reconciliation," when in fact the Greek has another word for reconciliation (*apokatallasso*).[48] The *apo* is always in the subjective genitive by default, which provides the prefix for the stem *kata* (down); it is always in the accusative, where accusation is made upon the subject; in this case the subject is attitude and in relation to deity. In an anthropomorphic sense, God throws down the gauntlet in terms of his relation to humankind. Then "Change" (-*allasso*) or causes it to become otherwise; hence we can translate it in the colloquial English "from change to a downright change." Consequently we can argue that God made a change to become otherwise, away from what Western thought has imposed upon the world, which is a depiction of a God who is deemed to be a narcissistic, belligerent bully, angry and bent on exacting revenge on his enemies who refuse to do his behest. Notwithstanding the inspiration of these postmodern mentalities pertinent within Western thought, God is Conciliated! This contradicts the notion that God is immutable. In what sense is this case? God is perfect in all of his contrivances and nothing can thwart his intention. He cannot change or mutate.[49] This is true, he remains constant. Therefore, his immutability of unchangeableness remains as aforesaid. Yet conciliation speaks of change from an offended party. In an anthropomorphic sense, God is the offended party member; in the sense of salvific history, he it is that is offended by mankind in their hostility and estrangement towards him.

The notion that has been framed in human minds is a distant God that is aloof and unmoved by human actions and sentiments; furthermore, the imagery that is projected of God is often distorted and false, and as such humankind is unable to accept that God can forgive heinous crimes and

---

47. Knoch, *Keyword Concordance*, 56.

48. Knoch, *Keyword Concordance*, 242.

49. James 1:17: "All good giving and every perfect gratuity is from above, descending from the Father of lights, in Whom that is no mutation or shadow from revolving motion." This is interesting as this epistle is considered the first letter written in the New Testament.

atrocities. Yet this is the pancreas that underpins Western soteriological thought. How then is God conciliated if he is immutable? God changes in the sense that his operation in relation to the cosmos is different; this is extrinsically seen, yet intrinsically He remains the same. He it is that provided that *shalom iréné* (peace) through His Son, Jesus the Christ, through his impeccable life and ultimate vicarious sacrificial atonement, publicly gibbeted at Golgotha. It is in this exhibition of love that condescended the supreme Deity to make the peace. That is, he is no longer offended extrinsically by the actions of humans. He is ironically conciliated, intrinsically as well as extrinsically. Thus, humans attempt to frustrate his intention for humankind, or use the shaking of the fist in the air as a gesture of one's offended and hostile attitude towards him.

Thus, I argue from the positive standpoint of salvation as praxis, that is, salvation as a metaphor for deliverance and redemption and as procurement for all mankind. Consequently, salvation then becomes pulchritude artistically, depicted in the beautification of the cross as the centerpiece of *eonian* salvation. Conciliation is the resultant act in which God is at peace with humanity, and humanity's response is to accept the peace and be reconciled. This is the notion that the Apostle Paul sought to elucidate within the Pauline corpus (e.g., 2 Cor 5:20).

The negative aspect suggests that this goes against the beautification of salvation, as its depiction of the triune God remains hostile to an unrepentant world, a world that refuses to accept the work of the cross. That is, one might say, "Free will will not permit me to make a choice for salvation as I am in control of my destiny. I make the choice of whether to receive or reject God. Salvation therefore is a human effort, a cooperation of God and human." This attitude says that salvation is not one-sided but it is a work of man and the Trinity.

It further contends that although common grace is available to all, special grace is for all who receive it.[50] Special grace is the metaphor in which the third person of the Godhead converts the sinner from dead works to righteousness; this is done as the active response of divine favor. McGrath suggests that this hypothesis of atonement and sacrifice is a notion that was born in the cultists of the Old Testament and was subsequently developed in the New Testament, and fleshed out in the early years of the patristic period.

---

50. Wayne Grudem coins this idea from his work, *Systematic Theology*, 657.

McGrath goes further. Through faith, believers participate in the risen Christ. They are "in Christ."[51] For McGrath, salvation is considered somewhat complex in its theoretical approaches; what he means by this is that salvation and its definition are not used in reference to a biblical theological trajectory. But also seculars utilize this, for McGrath argues from the standpoint that salvation is not just a Christian notion but that all religions offer some kind of salvation, as members of specific communities enjoy the benefit of liberation and freedom.[52] McGrath traverses through the gauntlet of how salvation theory was engaged from the traditions of the patristic period to the dawn of the enlightenment and beyond, to be engaged in postmodernism. In spite of the complexities involved, the narrative of salvation is still inextricably linked to the salvific redemptive work on the cross. This serves as the pendulum on which the door hinges for terms that provide the metaphors of redemption, deliverance, and other soteriological nuances; McGrath highlights these thoughts within the prism of the Pauline corpus, however, these metaphors are clearly elucidated that God will have all men be saved.[53]

The question is then: Is Western thought of salvation essentially philosophical in content, as it elucidates salvation through the prisms of human and scholastic thought as opposed to the biblical text? To answer the question, neo-liberalism understands the doctrine of salvation as a rebirth of a Christian. In the thoughts of Barth and Rahner, salvation is universal as opposed to eternal torment. Morwenna Ludlow provides a case for universal salvation as part of her PhD thesis *Universal Salvation* by looking at apocatastasis in the theology of Gregory of Nyssa to that of Karl Rahner. Her ability is to engage through the history and life of Gregory and his brother and sister Mercina, and then Rahner's response to universal salvation. The problematic issue for Rahner is criticism of scholars who viewed free will and salvation and of how these eschatological assertions are understood.[54]

---

51. McGrath argues that "Participating in Christ, is understood to mean forgiveness of sins, sharing in his righteousness. This we take it mean, becomes the central to Luther's soteriology, as his image of the marriage between Christ and the believers makes clear. In some way, faith unites us to Christ, and thus enables us to participate in his attributes" (McGrath, *Christian Theology*, 340).

52. This is devoid of any significant theological value, McGrath argues (*Christian Theology*, 327).

53. See McGrath's comments on this (*Christian Theology*, 350).

54. Ludlow asserts eschatology is Christology, anthropology, and sociology translated into an expectation of consummation. What was meant by Rahner assertions, Ludlow does not say, but it could be asserted that what was meant as Ludlow notes "the existence

UNIVERSAL SALVATION AS PRAXIS

Furthermore, Origen's *apokatastsis* says that grace is on the part of the devil and the damned, and this is so widespread that it has become one of those truths that no one can even think to verify.[55] Opposition to universal salvation contends that God is angry with humankind for their sin, and as such will mete out punishment for the ungodly and save those who through their respective free will will experience the bliss of salvation, and watch the damned in endless torment. The other view is an annexation in this, and contends that after judgment, the wicked will be annihilated. Only a remnant will enter into the kingdom and be saved. Selective salvation has held sway in Christendom for decades; it appears that this kept people in restraint for fear of eternal punishment and of losing their salvation.

Peterson seeks to make a case for eternal punishment by way of contrasting annihilation with destruction; he argues Paul's argument of destruction as "the wicked will be punished with everlasting destruction" (2 Thess 1:9).[56] Peterson further argues that God rules hell and his complete fury is unleashed against Satan, his angels, and wicked human beings.[57]

In Peterson's refutation of the doctrine of universal salvation, which he dubbed universalism, he rejects Hick's view that God will eventually succeed in His purpose of winning all men to Himself in faith and love. Peterson refutes Hicks's philosophical ground on which Hicks appealed. Therefore, Peterson sought to underplay the text that purports the argument of the salvation of all. In 1 Timothy 2:4, Paul did not teach that all will be saved in the end but that it is God's will for the gospel to reach everyone. To further buttress Peterson's argument, he contends that to rest on this text more would be an injustice to the rest of the context which speaks of final judgment and eternal torment. Thus universalism is unwarranted based on 1 Timothy 2:4.[58] Peterson further argues that the desires for all are to be saved, but he calls universalism a false teaching. In fact, because universal-

---

of the possibility that freedom will wend ion eternal loss stand alongside the doctrine that the world and the history of the as whole will in fact enter into eternal life with God" (Ludlow, *Universal Salvation*, 244–45).

55. Balthasar, *Dare We Hope that All Men Be Saved*, 42.

56. Peterson went further when he said, "Destruction is not a substitution for annhilationism, everlasting torment, it would be quite possible to understand 'death' 'destruction' and the like, as meaning a wrecked and ruined existence" (Peterson, *Hell on Trial*, 166).

57. Peterson says further, "The devil will be thrown in the lake of fire during with sulphur [and] tormented day and night for ever"(Rev 20:10) and wicked human beings will be tormented day and night" (Peterson, *Hell on Trial*, 187).

58. See Peterson, *Hell on Trial*, 153.

ism flies in the face of Scripture and deliberately avoids much of the biblical evidence, it is a sin to hold to it. He further argues that evangelical pity was well-founded, based as it was on the clear teaching of the redemption and of the apostles. Because universalism seeks to undermine the foundation, it must be rejected as evil.[59] Peterson gives three reasons why the doctrine of universal salvation (so-called universalism) should be refuted.[60]

Peterson's views are seen as the *sine qua non* of current Western views, which has helped shape the thinking of many evangelicals in Christendom. Salvation in Western thought is often seen as a hybrid of eternal torment and destruction. What appears difficult to engage is how is salvation lived within a Western context, as it appears that salvation is purely understood by all in the same way but there is more than one way that salvation is understood. Murphy contends that Eurocentric (Western) theology is a theoretical, abstract, and built-upon foundation of classical examination of revelation and tradition.[61] This is understood that white Western theology can be construed as the evaluation and analysis of European Christian thought; this deduction is then formulated and compounded into the epistemology that we now see expostulated in the current theological thinking.

Murphy further argues that the dogmatism of classical Western (white) theology has been the weapon of oppression for the people of African descent (this would include, I assume, American, Caribbean, and Asian, as well as British). Scholasticism, or classical Western theology is a system, both abstractive and logical, stressing what happens objectively: salvation of damnation and destruction. Modern contemporary theology is existential and personal, stressing what happens subjectively.[62] For this reason, its discursive narrative is void of a prophetic voice addressing the social and economic depression among the margins of the world.[63]

---

59. Peterson, 156.

60. He sought to engage with fundamentalist evangelicals like J. I. Packer, who argues that Christians' zeal in the eighteenth and nineteenth centuries was fueled by their love for hell-bound sinners. F. Torrence also states: "No doctrine of love, but only an abiding menace to the Gospel and to mankind, we then must replace the false universalism with what N.T Wright calls the "true Biblical Universal." This is the doctrine, which God and one way salvation to for all in Jesus Christ—This biblical 'universalism' gives the strongest motives for evangelism, namely the love of god and all men" (Peterson, 57).

61. Murphy, *Defining Salvation*, 33.

62. Murphy, *Defining Salvation*, 33.

63. Murphy argues that this empirical institutionalized white theology has failed both God and the people of the world. It is clear that salvation is defined in the context of white theology possessing power and wealth in order to fulfill a believed assigned divine

Universal Salvation as Praxis

In responding to Peterson, we note that this is the thinking that pervades white western thought; we have haggled that even Pentecostal evangelicals share a hybrid form of this, but not in its totality. Murphy's position is important and it is worth noting this theological disconnect as modern-day theologians uphold the established tone of inhumanity, injustice, and inequality when they fail to interpret the biblical message of salvation beyond power and economics.[64] Murphy further argues that white theology's definition of salvation appears void of biblical ethics, as well as equality.

Rousseau's definition of inequality tabulates the contradictions between Calvinism and biblical soteriology. The language of biblical theology challenges such embedded theological structures because Calvinism is void of humanity. Calvinistic theology has become a servant of the state, perpetuating the thought that salvation is only available to a select few, mainly whites, while denying others. This kind of theological hermeneutic is primarily of a private norm.[65]

Nevertheless, Murphy's contribution to salvation on behalf of all the families of the earth is important, and we should not eliminate this invaluable point. Nor should we make light of this fact that salvation has not worked for the darker peoples of the planet Earth, but only as befitted the Western thoughts and ideas, to the deterrent of the poor and oppressed peoples of the planet Earth. However, at the conclusion of the eons, salvation goes beyond our race. The salvation of all will readdress all the social ills and inequalities that have been heaped upon all the oppressed and marginalized people of the world. How this is done is not clearly elucidated in the biblical text. However, Scripture clearly points out that God will be all in all (1Cor 15:28)!

God will have all men be saved! This is His immutable plan that is unalterable. On the matter of race, we must bear in mind that God is a God of love, and as such His love transcend beyonds race, color, and nationality. At this present time, the tension of race and bigotry and narcissism will be abolished, to give way to life and shalom (peace). This appears to be a long way off, in the thinking of others who may be indifferent to these views. But the story of salvation is about the God of grace and love.

---

agenda (Murphy, *Defining Salvation*, 36).

64. Murphy, *Defining Salvation*, 39.

65. Murphy, *Defining Salvation*, 46–47.

CONCLUSION

The story of God's immutable plan is to help the reader understand the grace and love of God throughout the course of the eons. We sought to ascertain this by appealing to the minds of our readers. We spoke of God by taking a rather unorthodox position, yet we still painted the image of God in His divine theophany as a being who is unable to change, who sets out His plan according to His divine council, and there is nothing that thwarts His intention. Furthermore, theology is understood in this practical sense. We looked at Latin theology and how it changed the entire landscape of how theology is engaged within the prism of historical theology, up to the time of post-Enlightenment. We took a rather unorthodox position on Satan in the view that the faith of Satan is not clearly spelt out, but rather it is possible that Satan will be reconciled through the final subjection of all at the conclusion of the eons, when he would have served his purpose as an opponent to subjected creatures. The finer point on this matter is not clearly elucidated as this is a hypothesis; we do not have the final say in this regard. In regards to "eternal," the word is a foreign term to the sacred Scriptures and was part of the Latin theology to which our modern Bible based much of the language; therefore, it has no real place. We sought to clearly spell out the philology and the etymological usage of both the Hebrew and the Greek word eon, eons, and its adjective *eonian*, respectively, and concluded that the word in its original setting meant a limited duration. This we have argued should be used consistently, though biblical translators do not think this is the case; rather they would imply discordant rendering by translating it in a plethora of etymological ways to fit their own context. We agree that there is no such thing as a word-for-word translation. We are arguing for consistency, especially where this word is concerned. We looked at the word "hell," and have discovered that hell is a matter of how traditions are read as a backward trajectory into the Scriptures through philosophical ideas, backed by myths and legends.

We argue that salvation is an act of God, regardless of race. We are aware that the current issues of race and gender have caused more disparity than help. We have realized the sway and monopoly that Western thought has had since the dawn of the Enlightenment. Notwithstanding this, we contend that the pains of race and the pain of rejection and prejudice will be removed. We do not know how, but we do have a blessed hope that the elimination of hatred, bigotry, and narcissism will be ended and God will be all in all.

Bibliography

Bacon, Francis. *The Essays of Francis Bacon.* Edited by Mary Augusta Scott. http://www.people.virginia.edu/~jdk3t/Essays.pdf.
Baer, Jackson. *What the Hell: How Did We Get it So Wrong? Eternity, Grace, and the Message of Love.* Denver, CO: Outskirts, 2011.
Baker, Charles F. *A Dispensational Theology.* Grand Rapids, MI: Grace Bible College, 1986.
Balthasar, Hans Urs von. *Dare We Hope that All Men Be Saved?* Ignatius, 1986.
Barclay, William. *The Daily Study Bible,* 10 vols. Edinburgh: St. Andrew, 1975.
Barth, Karl. *The Epistle to the Romans.* Translated by E.C. Hoskins. Oxford: Oxford University Press, 1957.
Barton, John, and John Muddiman, eds. *The Oxford Bible Commentary.* Oxford: Oxford University Press, 2001.
Bauers, Walter. *Greek-English Lexicon of the New Testament.* Chicago: Chicago University Press, 1979.
Beauchemin, Gerry. *Hope Beyond Hell.* Olmito, TX: Malista, 2007.
Bengel, John. *New Testament Commentary.* Grand Rapids, MI: Kregel, 1982.
Berkhof, Louis. *Systematic Theology.* Edinburgh: Banner of Truth, 1976.
Biblia Hebraica Leningradensia and the King James Version. Peabody, MA: Hendrickson, 2003.
Biblia Hebraica Stutttgartensia and English Standard Version. Wheaton, IL: Crossway, 2012.
Black, Matthew, and H. H. Rowley, eds. *Peake's Commentary on the Bible.* New York: Routledge, 1997.
Bloesch, Donald G. *Essentials of Evangelical Theology.* Peabody, MA: Hendrickson, 2006.
Bonda, Jan. *The One Purpose of God.* Grand Rapids, MI: Eerdmans, 1998.
Bowles, Richard G. "Does Revelation 14:11 Teach Eternal Torment? Examining Proof Text on Hell." *Evangelical Quietly* 73.1 (2001) 21–36.
Bradley, Heath. *Flames of Love: Hell and Universal Salvation.* Eugene, OR: Wipf & Stock, 2012.
Brown, Colin. *Dictionary of New Testament Theology,* 4 vols. Grand Rapids, MI: Zondervan, 2003.
Brown, Francis, ed. *Hebrew and English Lexicon of the Old Testament.* Oxford: Oxford University Press, 1952.
Brüggemann, Walter. *The Prophetic Imagination.* Minneapolis: Fortress, 2001.
Bultmann, Rudolf. *Theology of the New Testament.* Waco, TX: Baylor University Press, 2007.

Bibliography

Burnfield, David. *Patristic Universalism*. Boca Raton, FL: Universal, 2013.
Buttrick, George A. *The Interpreter's One-Volume Commentary on the Bible*. Nashville, TN: Abingdon, 1971.
Calvin, John. *The Institutes of the Christian Religion*. Edited and translated by Henry Beveridge. Peabody, MA: Hendrickson, 1974.
———. *The Institutes of the Christian Religion*. Edited by John T. McNeill and translated by Fred Lewis Battles. London: Westminster Press, 1960.
Carson, Donald A. *The Difficult Doctrine Of Love*. Wheaton, IL: Crossway, 2000.
Carson, Donald A., and Greg K. Beale, eds. *A Commentary on the New Testament Use of the Old Testament*. Grand Rapids, MI: Baker, 2007.
Chamberlain, Mark T., and Thomas Allin. *Every Knee Shall Bow*. Xulon, 2005.
Christian Standard Bible. Nashville, TN: Holman Bible Publishers, 2017.
Coltfelter, David. *Sinners in the Hands of a Good God: Reconciling Divine Judgment and Mercy*. Chicago: Moody, 2004.
Common English Bible. Nashville, TN: Church Resources Development, 2001.
Companion Bible KJV. Grand Rapids, MI: Kregel, 1990.
Coogan, Michael, ed. *The New Oxford Annotated Bible*. Oxford: Oxford University Press, 2010.
Cox, Samuel. *Salvator Mundi:* Almont, MI: Saviour of All Fellowship, 1990.
Craig, William Lane. "On the Possibility of Eternal Damnation." *Religious Studies* 28.2 (1992) 495–510.
———. *The Only Wise God*. Eugene, OR: Wipf & Stock, 2000.
Crossen, John Dominic. *The Power of Parable: How Fiction by Jesus Became Fiction about Jesus*. San Francisco: HarperOne, 2012.
Dunn, James D.G., ed. *Eerdmans Commentary of the Bible*. Grand Rapids, MI: Eerdmans, 2003.
English Standard Version. Wheaton, IL: Crossway, 2011.
Enns, Paul P. *The Moody Handbook of Theology*. Chicago: Moody, 2008.
Freedman, David Noel, et al. *Anchor Bible Dictionary*, vol. 6. New York: Doubleday, 1992.
Fudge, Edward William. *The Fire That Consumes*. Eugene, OR: Wipf & Stock, 2011.
Geisler, Norman L. *Chosen But Free*. Minneapolis, MN: Bethany House, 2001.
Girdlestone, Robert B. *Synonyms of the Old Testament*. Grand Rapids, MI: Eerdmans, 1986.
Gray, Tony. "Hell in the Twentieth Century." *Epworth Review* 23.1 (1996) 28–32.
Grudem, Wayne. *Systematic Theology: An Introduction to Biblical Doctrine*. Grand Rapids, MI: Zondervan, 1994.
Gulley, Philip, and James Mulholland. *If Grace is True: Why God Will Save Every Person*. San Francisco: HarperOne, 2004.
Gundry, Stanley, et al., eds. *Four Views on Hell*. Counterpoints: Bible and Theology. Grand Rapids, MI: Zondervan, 1996.
Hanson, John Wesley. *The Greek Word Aion-Aionios Translated Everlasting-Eternal*. Chicago: Northwestern Universalist, 1875.
———. *Universalism the Prevailing Doctrine of the Christian Church During Its First Five Hundred Years*. Amazon Digital Services, 2014.
Hodge, Charles. *Systematic Theology*, 3 vols. Grand Rapids, MI: Eerdmans, 1986.
Holladay, William L. *A Concise Hebrew and Aramaic Lexicon of the Old Testament*. Grand Rapids, MI: Eerdmans, 1988.
Holman Christian Standard Bible. Nashville, TN: Holman Bible, 2009.

BIBLIOGRAPHY

Jeremias, Joachim. *Rediscovering the Parables*. London: SCM, 1966.
Jersak, Bradley. *Her Gates Will Never Be Shut: Hope, Hell, and the New Jerusalem*. Eugene, OR: Wipf & Stock, 2009.
Jongkind, Dirk. "Introduction." In *The Greek New Testament* by Tyndale House 1–30. Cambridge, UK: Crossway, 2017.
Keathley, Kenneth. *Salvation Sovereignty: A Molinist Approach*. Nashville, TN: B&H, 2010.
Keizer, Helena Maria. *Life Time Entirety: A Study of AIΩN in Greek Literature and Philosophy, the Septuagint and Philo*. PhD diss, University of Amsterdam, 1999.
Kendall, R. T. *Once Saved Always Saved*. Milton Keynes, UK: Paternoster, 1983.
Kittel, Gerhard, ed. *Theological Dictionary of the New Testament*, 10 vols. Translated by Geoffrey Bromiley. Grand Rapids, MI: Eerdmans, 2006.
Knoch, A.E. *All in All: The Goal of the Universe*. Santa Clarita, CA: Concordant, 1978.
———. *Concordant Commentary on the New Testament*. Santa Clarita, CA: Concordant, 1968.
———. *Keyword Concordance to the Concordant Commentary*. Santa Clarita, CA: Concordant, 1968.
———. *The Problem of Evil and the Judgements of God*. Santa Clarita, CA: Concordant, 1976.
———. *The Rich Man and Lazarus*. Santa Clarita, CA: Concordant, 1960.
———. *Substitution or Inclusion*. Santa Clarita, CA: Concordant, 1997.
Knoch, A. E., ed. *Concordant Literal New Testament*. Santa Carita, CA: Concordant, 1983.
Knoch, A.E., et al., eds. *Unsearchable Riches*, 70 vols. Santa Clarita, CA: Concordant, 1900–2000.
Kronen, John, and Eric Reitan. *God's Final Victory: A Comparative Philosophical Case for Universalism*. London: Bloomsbury, 2011.
Longman, Thrempter, III. *The Baker Illustrated Bible Dictionary*. Grand Rapids, MI: Baker, 2013.
Ludlow, Morwenna. *Universal Salvation: Eschatology in the Thought of Gregory of Nyssa and Karl Rahner*. Oxford Theology and Religion Monographs. Oxford: Oxford University Press, 2009.
Luther, Martin. *The Bondage of the Will*. Translated by O. R. Johnston and J. I. Packer. Grand Rapids, MI: Baker, 2012.
McGrath, Alister. *Christian Theology: An Introduction*. London: Blackwell, 2007.
Mill, John Stuart. *Liberty*. London: Epworth, 1975.
Mills, Watson E. *Lutterworth Dictionary of the Bible*. London: James Clarke, 1994.
Morgan, G. Campbell. *Parables and Metaphors of our Lord*. London: Marshall, Morgan & Scott, 1943.
Morgan, Christopher W., ed. *Is Hell for Real or Does Everyone Go To Heaven?* Grand Rapids, MI: Zondervan, 2004.
Moulton, J. H., and George Milligan. *The Vocabulary of the Greek New Testament*. London: Hodder & Stoughton, 1929.
Mounce, William D. *Complete Expository Dictionary of Old and New Testament Words*. Grand Rapids, MI: Zondervan, 2006.
Muller, Richard A. *Dictionary of Latin and Greek Theological Terms: Drawn Principally from Protestant Scholastic Theology*. Grand Rapids, MI: Baker, 1985.
Murphy, James T., Jr. *Defining Salvation in the Context of Black Theology*. Xlibris, 2012.
Nestle-Aland Novum Testamentum Latine. Gesmtherstellung: Nördlingen, 1989.
Nestle-Aland Novum Testamentum Graece. Deutche Bibelgellschaft, 2013.

Bibliography

New American Standard. Nashville, TN: Nelson, 1977.
New International Version. Grand Rapids, MI: Zondervan, 2002.
O'Collins, Gerald. *Salvation for All: God's Other Peoples.* Oxford: Oxford University Press, 2008.
Packer, J. I. *'Fundamentalism' and the Word of God.* Grand Rapids, MI: Eerdmans, 1958.
Parry, Robin, and Christopher Partridge, eds. *Universal Salvation? The Current Debate.* Grand Rapids, MI: Eerdmans, 2003.
Peart, Charles. *God Rules for Scriptural Interpretation.* Santa Clarita, CA: Concordant, 1956.
Peterson, Robert A. *Election and Free Will.* Phillipsburg, NJ: P&R, 2007.
———. *Hell on Trial: The Case for Eternal Punishment.* Phillipsburg, NJ: P&R, 1995.
Plantinga, Alvin. *Good, Freedom and Evil.* Grand Rapids, MI: Eerdmans, 1974.
Polliout, S H. "Article#57: Eternal or Eonian?" http://www.kingdomandglory.com/art/art57.html.
Ramelli, Ilari, and David Konstan. *Terms For Eternity: Aiônios and Aïdios in Classical and Christian Texts.* Piscataway, NJ: Gorgias, 2007.
Revised Standard Version. London: Oxford University Press, 1971.
Robertson, Archibald T. *Word Pictures of the New Testament,* 6 vols. Grand Rapids, MI: Baker, 1930.
Robinson, Maurice, and Mark House. Robinson and House, *Analytical Lexicon of the New Testament.* Peabody, MA: Hendrickson, 2012.
Rosner, Brian S., et al. *New Dictionary of Biblical Theology.* Downers Grove, IL: IVP, 2000.
Sakenfield, Katherine Doob. *The Interpreters Dictionary of the Bible,* 5 vols. Nashville, TN: Abingdon, 2009.
Snodgrass, Klyne R. *Stories with Intent: A Comprehensive Guide to the Parables of Jesus.* Grand Rapids, MI: Eerdmans, 2008.
Stanford University Encyclopedia of Philosophy. https://plato.stanford.edu/.
Stern, David H. *Jewish New Testament Commentary.* Clarksville, MD: Jewish New Testament, 1994.
Stetson, Eric. *Christian Universalism: God's Good News for All People.* Sparkling Bay, 2008.
Stevenson, G.T. *Time and Eternity.* Almont, MI: Saviour of All Fellowship, 1989.
Strauss, Mark L. "Form, Function and the "Literal Meaning" Fallacy in English Translation." *The Bible Translator.* United Bible Societies 56.3 (July 2005).
Talbott, Thomas. "Of Divine Foreknowledge and Bringing about the Past." *Philosophy and Phenomenological Research* 46.3 (1986) 455–69.
———. *The Inescapable Love of God.* Eugene, OR: Cascade, 2014.
———. *The Inescapable Love of God.* Boca Raton, FL: Universal, 1999.
———. "The Love of God and Heresy of Exclusivism." *Christian Scholars' Review* 27 (1997) 30–56.
———. "Punishment, Forgiveness, and Divine Justice." *Religious Studies* 29.2 (1993) 151–68.
———. "Universal Reconciliation and the Inclusive Nature of Election." https://pdfs.semanticscholar.org/4231/4d3d7c2cb153e82b30c9ecd1794c31e7458a.pdf.
———. "The Just Mercy of God: Universal Salvation in the Theology of George MacDonald (1824–1905)." *Evangelical Review* 72:1 (2001).
Tate, W. Randolph. *Handbook for Biblical Interpretation: An Essential Guide to Methods, Terms, and Concepts.* Grand Rapids, MI: Baker, 2006.

BIBLIOGRAPHY

Tayler, Bernard, ed. *Analytical Lexicon to the Septuagint*. Peabody, MA: Hendrickson, 2009.
Thomson, Alexander. *Whence Eternity*. Santa Clarita, CA: Concordant, 1956.
Tillich, Paul. *Systematic Theology*, 3 vols. London: Nisbet, 1968.
Toorn, Karel van der, et al., eds. *Dictionary of Deities and Demons in The Bible*. Grand Rapids, MI: Erdmanns, 1999.
VanGemeren, Willem A., ed. *Dictionary of Old Testament Theology and Exegesis*, 4 vols. Grand Rapids, MI: Zondervan, 1997.
Vines, W.E. *New Testament Greek Grammar and Dictionary*. Nashville, TN: Nelson, 2012.
Walls, Jerry L. *Heaven, Hell and Purgatory*. Grand Rapids, MI: Brazos, 2015.
Whitaker, Richard E., and James E. Gohring. *The Eerdmans Analytical Concordance to the Revised Standard Version of the Bible*. Grand Rapids, MI: Eerdmans, 1988.
Wolff, Christian. "The Existence of God, Natural Theology." *International Journal for Philosophy of Religion* 4 (1973) 105–18.
Wright, David F., et al., eds. *New Dictionary of Theology*. Downers Grove, IL: IVP, 2016.

www.ingramcontent.com/pod-product-compliance
Lightning Source LLC
Chambersburg PA
CBHW071444160426
43195CB00013B/2024